Say That the River Turns
The Impact of Gwendolyn Brooks

BOOKS BY HAKI R. MADHUBUTI

Poetry

Think Black
Black Pride
Don't Cry, Scream
We Walk the Way of the New World
Directionscore: Selected and New Poems
Book of Life
Earthquakes and Sunrise Missions
Killing Memory, Seeking Ancestors

Essays

Enemies: The Clash of Races
From Plan to Planet, Life Studies: The Need for Black Minds and Institutions
A Capsule Course in Black Poetry Writing (co-authored with Gwendolyn Brooks, Keorapetse Kgositsile, and Dudley Randall)
Black Men: Obsolete, Single, Dangerous? The Afrikan American Family in Transition
Dynamite Voices: Black Poets of the 1960's

Edited

Confusion By Any Other Name: The Negative Impact of the Blackman's Guide to Understanding the Blackwoman
To Gwen, With Love (edited with Francis Ward and Patricia L. Brown)
Say That The River Turns: The Impact of Gwendolyn Brooks

Records/Tapes

Rappin and Readin
Rise Vision Coming
    (with the Afrikan Liberation Arts Ensemble)

Say That the River Turns
The Impact of Gwendolyn Brooks

Edited by Haki R. Madhubuti

Chicago
Third World Press

First edition
Second printing 1990

Cover Photograph by Addo Carpenter
Book design by SERIF, Ltd.

ISBN: 0-88378-118-2

Manufactured in the United States of America
Third World Press
7524 S. Cottage Grove Ave.
Chicago, IL 60619

Dedication

To
Hoyt W. Fuller
David Llorens
George E. Kent
Alice Browning

and

To the contributers of this volume. Without their words and images, *Say that the River Turns: The Impact of Gwendolyn Brooks* would have been but a dream.

Contents

The Woman, The Work, The Music

Introduction: Gwendolyn Brooks at 70
Haki R. Madhubuti

> My people, black and black, revile the
>   River.
> Say that the River Turns, and turn the
>   River.

These are magical lines, somewhat like marching orders. Gwendolyn Brooks has been a formidable literary example for nearly two generations. Her impact is unquestionably enormous. Few other African-American writers since Langston Hughes have influenced such a large and diverse readership.

On June 7, 1987 Ms. Brooks turned seventy and like the River, she, in her quiet manner, can look back over a lifetime of working with language and see her many turnings. Her motion has indeed been riverlike, a force of nature that is both unpredictable and dependable, strong and life-giving. Her place in world literature is secure and notable. However her greatest impact has been as key player in the literature of African-American people.

With the publication of her collected works *Blacks* (1987), in one massive volume, we see the life production of a serious mind. Her concern has been for clarity and precise utterance that demand a response from readers. Her work represents a waterfall, a gigantic contribution that connects her vision to possibilities. It is in the work of Langston Hughes, Margaret Walker, Sterling Brown and Gwendolyn Brooks that one begins to understand what it means to be a writer of the people. At seventy years young she is a Living National Treasure. Although her work is often analyzed for its literary value, it is also infused with a spiritual force in which one can see the secret to her longevity. That spiritual force has to do with a passion for the truth within the truth. Her search goes beyond that which most people see and accept.

In academia it has been stated more than once that "most literary forms are artificial" and that they change with the "tone and mood of the culture." Within the poetry of Ms. Brooks we see profound originality. This has been her mainstay. Her mind, ever fresh, reminds us of how a tenth generation computer might work. She has created form to fit an urban content. The major difference between people who write and serious writers is *originality* and *vision.* From *A Street in Bronzville* (1945) to the *Near-Johannes-burg Boy* (1986) we are able to read a writer whose telling of the African-American story is a delicate dance between structure and content. She stated in 1973 that "my aim, in my next future, is to write poems that will somehow successfully 'call' all black people: black people in taverns, black people in alleys, black people in gutters, schools, offices, factories, prisons, the consulate; I wish to reach black people in pulpits, black people in mines, on farms, on thrones; Not always to 'teach'—I wish often to entertain, to illumine." She has succeeded. Her readings, whether at universities or community centers, are packed with the spirit of her people.

However, it is in her vision—her ability to see truths rather than trends, to seek meaning and not fads, to question ideas rather than gossip—that endears her to us. Her uniqueness with language is common knowledge and few would argue with the fact that she has helped to set new standards for poetry in the twentieth century. She is a slow and careful writer. In the totality of her work there is little that will not stand the test of close, critical examination.

Ms. Brooks' strength is in both form and ideas. She is a cultural writer and she makes the reader work. The experience and knowledge that she transmits is as full and as rich as the artistic brilliance of Duke Ellington, John Coltrane, Charles White, Romare Bearden, Gordon Parks, Elizabeth Catlett and Katherine Dunham.

Ms. Brooks' work, as this anthology suggests, means a great deal to a lot of writers. She is the standard which most of us use to measure our development. She is the writer who other writers buy to send to writers. She is the writer who many of us use in writers workshops and literature courses. She has the statue of a Queen Mother, but is always assessable and giving. Ms. Brooks is a woman who cannot live without her art, but who has never put her art above or before the people she writes about. And because of her art she has gained unlimited acceptance among a great many of the world's people.

This tribute was developed in a very short period of time. Herein are a group of writers and visual artists who are singing thank you. They are pieces from the heart, for Gwendolyn Brooks' love has been unlimited, her poetry inspiring, and her presence unparalleled. We have all grown because of her.

POET: Gwendolyn Brooks at 70   *Haki R. Madhubuti*

as in music,
as in griots singing,
as in language mastered, matured
beyond melodic roots.

you came from the land of ivory and vegation,
of seasons with large women guarding secrets,
your father was a running mountain,
your mother a crop-gatherer and God-carrier,
your family, earthgrown waterfalls,
all tested, clearheaded, focused,
ready to engage.

centuries displaced in this land of denial and disbelief,
this land of slavery and sugar diets,
of bacon breakfasts, short suns and long moons,
you sought memory and hidded ideas,
while writing the portrait of a battered people.

artfully you avoided becoming a literary museum,
side-stepped retirement and canonization,
gently casting a rising shadow over a generation of
urgent-creators waiting to make fire,
make change.

with the wind in your hand,
as in trumpeter blowing,
as in poet singing,
as in sister of the people, of the language,
smile at your work.

your harvest is coming in boutifully.

Haki and Gwendolyn

MAIL ROOM
DO NOT ENTER
MAIL CAN BE DROPPED OFF
AND PICKED UP BETWEEN:
10:00AM-11:00AM
1:00 PM-2:00PM
NOTHING
OR AFTER

The Message

Of Flowers and Fire and Flowers
Gwendolyn Brooks

What's happening in black poetry now? Chained churning. Outright "flowers." Interested mumblings. SOME revolution-oriented vigor!

About late Sixties' poetry I was able to say: "The new black ideal italicizes black identity, black solidarity, and black self-address." It was a clean delight to be able to say that. It was good to be able to say: "Furthermore, the *essential* black ideal vitally acknowledges Afrikan roots."

In the late Sixties, it seemed to me, there *had* to be an accented recognition of new understandings; there *had* to be, for example, comprehension of the fact that shrieking into the steady and organized deafness of the white ear was frivolous. "There were things to be said to black brothers and sisters, and these things, annunciatory, curative, inspiriting, were to be said forthwith, without frill and without fear of the white presence. There was impatience with idle embroidery, with what was considered avoidance—avoidance of the gut issue, the blood fact. Literary rhythms altered. Sometimes the literature seemed to issue from pens dipped in, *stabbed* in, writhing blood. Music was very important. It influenced the new pens. There were switches from Benny Goodman to John Coltrane and Charlie Mingus—from 'I'll Be Seeing You' to 'Soulful Strut'. . . .

The best poems of the late Sixties were Arrivals. Much of the black poetry you read today is Going Somewhere. Where? The poets themselves are not always "sure" of their destination. Well, that's exciting. *We* don't know and *they* don't know what's to happen next. . . .

The Forties and Fifties were years of high poet-incense; the language-flowers were thickly sweet. Those flowers whined and begged white folks to pick them, to find them lovable. Then—the Sixties: independent fire!

Well, I don't want us to creep back to the weaker flowers of the old yesterday. I don't want us to subscribe, again, to Shelley or

Pound-Eliot or Wallace Stevens. I don't want us to forget the Fire. Baldwin's announced "Next Time" is by no means over. I want us to "advance," yes, to experiment, yes, to labor, yes. But I don't want us to forget the Fire.

From *Black Books Bulletin*
Volume 3, Fall 1975

Inside Track on Evans Avenue

How I Met Miss Brooks
Henry Blakely

It all began on a hayride.

There were only two Blacks (Negroes in those days) on the *Wilson Press*, the school newspaper at Wilson Junior College in Chicago. The two Blacks were Sarah M. and myself. Black, and male and female. Whenever Wilson Press assembled for things social or off-campus, Sarah and I were automatically paired.

This was not onerous; Sarah was attractive and easy to talk to. She had three brothers and knew how to deal with foot-in-mouth males. Talking to girls had always been a problem. I had two brothers, no sisters, and Tilden Prevocational followed by Tilden Tech had not broadened my conversatonal skills. Arm wrestling, betting that you could lift the front end of a Model T higher than anyone else, was not coin in the new realm. Wilson Junior College, with all its pretty girls, was Nirvana and confusion.

And so I went to my favorite aunt. "Aunt Mary," I asked, "what do you talk about to girls?"

"You talk to them about things that interest you," she said.

That was too easy. Years were to pass before I appreciated the great woman's wisdom.

Strangely, it would not have been as easy to go to my mother with that sort of question. Mother was ambivalent about her sons and maturity. She wanted good men but without a father in the home, boys were easier to raise. Her family and conventional wisdom were responsible for this feeling. "A single woman can't raise three boys in Chicago," too many voices had said.

For cases of severe arrested social development in the too carefully raised games like postoffice spanned ineptitudes. One didn't need booster shots of bourbon or cocaine when there was postoffice. I recall being more unsuccessful than usual at one ineptitude-spanning opportunity. I could not drag a reluctant female into the "postoffice" closet. She seemed warmly approachable but she just wouldn't be postofficed. Some of my buddies commented cruelly on my lack of success. Only later did I learn that she was the mother of the hostess.

Almost as good as postoffice were the infrequent and daring times at Wilson when several friends and I would chase cooperating girls up four flights in the domed building, catch them and carry them squealing four flights down, then turn them loose and chase them back up again. One of my male peers saw us one day and was condescendingly amused. I learned that he later fathered a child by one of the girls. He had not been catching them and turning them loose to run free and be caught again.

Mother had done well by us there. You did not do things like that to girls you would not want to marry, and you would not do things like that to girls you would want to marry. "Girls were flowers," mother said.

Girls were flowers and fauns and all things lovely. I remember one summer evening. Lola on the first floor of the two-story frame on 64th and Langley where we lived, was being visited by a creature whose skin was the color of peach and whose hair blew in the wind. I was nineteen; it was darkening but not dark. Mother came down.

"I'm going out, go on upstairs and go to bed," she said.

I gathered myself to obey and then "No" I said. "You go on, Mother." She looked at me, pursed her mouth as when thinking, said something about not staying out too late, nodded a greeting to the girls and then down the porch steps toward 65th for a walk over to Cottage Crove and the streetcar. I grew a little that evening; mother never again told me when to go to bed.

She didn't quite see me as ready to "loney" though, her word for making it on one's own. And when at almost twenty-three I was engaged to be married, she told my future in-laws I was still playing with motorcyles and guns as in my teen years.

Lola's visitor, Pearl, became my first serious girlfriend. She was seventeen and had a nineteen year old niece. The niece always chaperoned us, eagle-eyed and ten steps behind on Sunday walks from Pearl's home up Evans to 69th and back again. I called Alvin, a friend, to get her out of my hair. Alvin was furious when he realized I had called him to see a girl, not a car. But he joined in the Sunday walks and car rides and as of this year, 1987, they have been married 49 years.

As for myself and Pearl, she, natural, sweet, may have found me stuffy, and I was discovering that for me, mind quality was the thing I most appreciated in women.

After the Wilson College days Ernest Price dropped by one

Sunday. My brothers and I had just finished overhauling the family car and I invited Ernest to go for a test drive. OK, he said but first he'd have to stick his head in the church door because he'd told his parents he was going to BYPU (Baptist Young Peoples Union). I agreed to touch that base with him and then we'd be on our way. We never really had that test drive. I went to the Berean Church BYPU that Sunday and every Sunday thereafter for more than two years. Ernest, my schoolmate, and later my business partner for most of his working lifetime, had an early death at age 56.

Sarah was also a member of the Berean BYPU. In addition to character developing assignments such as giving a talk on life insurance to the regular Sunday evening service (I had just gotten my license and a job), there were parties and picnics and wonder of wonders, a hayride. Mrs. Bradshaw, in charge of BYPU, planned that hayride. Knowing Sarah better than any of the other girls, once again we were thrown together. I mean thrown literally. In our Wilson College days we had never had such head-on propinquity. And soon a disturbing fact became evident. There was boy and girl and bond but no chemistry. Bond? After almost 50 years whenever I see Sarah, although I may say no more than 'Hi!' I am deeply glad; she is a part of my good life.

"We aren't getting anywhere, are we?" I was apologetic.

"No," she said, "but I didn't what to hurt your feelings."

The other revelers seemed to be enjoying themselves. After a moment of silence, Sarah said, "I know just the girl for you." And she told me about a shy brown girl who attended Junior NAACP meetings and wrote poetry.

I was present at the next Junior NAACP meeting. Margaret Taylor, later to be Margaret Taylor Goss Burroughs, and finally, Dr. Burroughs, was seated beside Miss Brooks. "Hey Boy!" she called out as I walked past to take a seat further forward, "This girl wants to meet you." Dar irrepressible Margaret.

Miss Brooks had to give a report of some sort. A dress longish and brown hung loosely on her slim, brown frame. Her voice, despite her shyness, was rich and deep. I sensed through that voice that almost all of her shining was inward, and I felt warm in that shining. Miss Brooks later told me that on seeing me she confided to Margaret, "That's the man I'm going to marry."

And so, to conclude a story grown overlong in the telling, that is how I met Miss Brooks.

THREE-WAY MIRROR
Nora Brooks Blakely

"What's it like? Having Gwendolyn Brooks for a mother?"—is the often-asked question.

"I don't know. I've never had another mother to compare her to!"—is the semi-flip reply.

And yet, even without an opportunity for comparison shopping, there *are* differences. Most people get to see their mothers as, well—as *mothers*. They may be peripherally aware of a career she has OUT THERE, but it doesn't really connect with their corner of reality. I get to see mama in many different guises.

MAMA AS MADWOMAN

Many people see Gwendolyn Brooks as a shy, retiring, *quiet* sort of person. As her daughter I know the truth—and will now expose it.

Miss Brooks watches soap operas (yes, she does!) and usually does not answer her phone while they are on. One time I called and she said, "All My Children," and hung up.

As I was growing up my mother would dance through the house, hands high over her head, to the sounds of Errol Garner on television. She loved to play the piano and would beat out Duke Ellington songs like "Mood Indigo" or "Solitude" while I draped myself over the piano, vamp-style, and sang.

This "quiet" person is the one who gossips and giggles with me on the phone, often for two or three hours at a time, talking about everything from the cataclysmic to the comic. The phone is not her only avenue of communication. My mother is a "clipaholic." She cuts clippings out of newspapers by the truckload. When I was a child I used to find these clippings attached to my bedroom mirror. After I moved away from home she would collect bundles of them that would lie in wait, on the living room radiator until I came over. In recent years she has started mailing me clippings from out-of-town newspapers while she's on the road. I have now faced facts. If I take up residence on the moon, the next shuttle will contain clippings from my mother.

MAMA AS MIDWIFE

Gwendolyn Brooks has always been interested in assisting in the birth and development of new writers. In the '60s she was a focal point for most of the young Black writers in Chicago and across the country. Our house became a regular meeting place and think tank. She thrives on the informal sessions she has on myriad college campuses talking not only about literature, but also "The World." Her mail is filled with the letters of people she has touched.

She has been a firm believer in the phrase "give 'til it hurts." For years she went around the country giving grants to individual students, offering awards, and even creating contests at schools, until she could no longer afford it. My father and I started calling her "Our Lady of the Open Mouth," because of the numerous times she got excited about an idea or a person and volunteered her funds.

Most important of all, however, is her affect on children, through the schools she visits and the Illinois Poet Laureate Awards. Every year hundreds of poems pour in from elementary and high school students all over the state. She *alone* judges the poems, and pays for the awards *out of her own pocket*. Annually the winners get awards of $50 each, but she gets an award, too: the "up-faced" excitement of parents and children alike.

MAMA AS "MAPPER"

More than anything else, though, my mother is a "mapper." She delineates and defines the scenery of now. Her words are a mirror-flection of the "aroundness." Her poetic people are friends and acquaintances that command instant recognition:

> you say—"I know Big Bertha, Pepita and Nerissa."
> you say—"I feel for the 'Near-Johannesburg Boy.'"
> you say—"I've *been* that 'crazy woman.'"
> you say—"Lincoln West is a friend of mine."

Gwendolyn Brooks introduces and shares experiences. When she says "the only sanity is a cup of tea" you recognize a Truth. Little girls' songs; the "grayed in and gray"-ness of the day-to-day; animals grazing; computers; the fact that "we are each others' business," and the need to "conduct our blooming in the noise and

8

whip of the whirlwind,"—these are all entrances to the lives of people you might, otherwise, never know.

Gwendolyn, whether as manic parent, literary midwife, or life mapper opens places for people—new doorways and mindpaths.

And, after all, isn't that what a mother is supposed to do?

Gwendolyn and Nora

Beyond Mecca

My Friend Gwen
Margaret Burroughs

It is indeed a priviledge for me to have the opportunity to share some thoughts with other friends about my friend "Gwen." I am honored that Gwen and Henry have been my friends for over 50 years!

Early memories... Gwendolyn, Henry, Robert McGee, Evelyn Ganns, Joe Quinn and I and others were all members of the Chicago N.A.A.C.P. Youth Council. Frances Taylor Moseley, now Matlock, was our Sponsor. We met weekly under her guidance at the Y.W.C.A. on the northeast corner of 46th and South Parkway (now King Drive). It is an empty lot now. One of our main concerns at that time was to "stop lynching," and to "save the Scottsboro boys." One Saturday, we planned a demonstration march. We painted our own picket signs and set out on our march led by our beautiful young sponsor.

We started at 43rd and South Parkway (now King Drive) and walked west to State Street, then south on State to 47th Street. We marched east on 47th Street to King. Then we marched south on King to 51st Street. At each intersection Robert McGee (now a minister), would plop down his soapbox and jump up on it. For several minutes while we cheered and egged him on. Robert would preach and rail against lynching. The people who were passing stopped to listen to what we young people were up to. When Robert finished, we all cheered and applauded and the onlookers joined in. Then Robert picked up the soapbox and we went on to the next stop. At about 47th and Vincennes Avenue we were stopped by the police who asked if we had a permit. We did not. The whole raggle taggle group of us, including Gwen, Henry and myself, might have been hustled off to jail. However, our sponsor, Mrs. Mosley, charmed and talked them out of it.

Then, there were the poetry classes that Gwen and Henry and I attended at the South Side Community Art Center on 38th and Michigan Avenue. Our teacher was a very warm, sincere and affluent white woman named Inez Cunningham Stark, who lived in a condo on the near north side. She was on the board of *Poetry* magazine. Each Wednesday evening she would come to the South

Side and critique our poetry and prose writings. Gwen Brooks was the shining star of that class. Also in the class were Henry, Margaret Danner, Robert Davis, and several others. I remember the poetry contest that Mrs. Boulton had for us. S.I. Hayahawa was one of the judges. Gwendolyn won the first prize. I won the second. Henry won the third and Robert Davis won the fourth prize. Now, we all were not in the least surprised that Gwen won first prize. We knew back then that hers was a real talent. We felt that it was just a matter of time before all of Chcago, all of the country would discover what we knew about Gwen.

Thus, when Gwen honed and perfected her talents and all of the honors and recognitions began to be showered on her, we were not surprised. We knew it all the time.

Years had passed and it was in the seventies. I was on the Continent. I was visiting in Dakar, Senegal. I was sitting in the patio of the New Africa Hotel. Suddenly, I heard my name called. It was a familiar voice. It was none other than my friend Gwen. I hadn't expect her to be in Africa! You cannot imagine what a thrill it is to run unexpectedly into an old friend from home there in the homeland. Well, Gwen and I really had a reunion! Yes, we did!

I am very, very proud of my friend Gwen. She is indeed our 20th Century Phyllis Wheatley. Gwen is a pride and a joy of our people. My life among others has been enriched and strengthened by my long time friendship with both Gwendolyn and Henry. May the Gods of our fathers continue to smile upon them both.

The Soul of Gwendolyn Brooks
Lerone Bennett Jr.

She not only writes poems but she *is* a poem.

She is, as I have said, "grace in free verse . . . she is a sermon, she is a rhyme, a rhythm, a Reality."*

She taught me, she taught us, she taught a whole generation how to see, how to say, how to *Gwen*dolyn. And what we honor here is not the word alone but the word fed by the blood of the spirit. Let there be no misunderstanding on that point. For Gwendolyn Brooks is, to paraphrase one of her poems, the real thing. In an age of instant celebrities, instant artists and instant solutions, she is a long-distance runner who reminds us of the greatness and the grandeur of our task.

She has been on the road a long time now, fighting lions and tigers and the dragons of success and racism, and she tells us today in the beauty of her seventy years that "no daring is fatal." That's what she tells us. She tells us that the darkness is light enough and that the Black light we reflect is almost the only light left.

And let us not make the mistake here of fragmenting her life. For she has always been committed and lyrical and relevant. Before it was fashionable, before it was profitable, she was tone deep in Blackness. In the fifties, she was writing poems about Emmett Till and Little Rock and the Black boys and girls who came North looking for the Promised Land and found concrete deserts. In fact, she has always written about the sounds, sights and flavors of the Black community. And her poems are characterized by a bittersweet lyricism and an overwhelming concreteness.

Like Duke Ellington, like Charlie Parker, like the griots of Africa and the poets of slavery, she is elegant and earthy. Her poems are filled with names like Big Bessie, Mrs. Martin's Booker T., Mae Belle and Pearl May Lee, with images of broken bottles and roses in whiskey glasses, with "illegible landlords," rooms full of beads and receipts, and love in the crowding darkness of the South Side at midnight in May. ("When you have, I say, forgotten all that/ Then you may tell,/ Then I may believe/ You have forgotten me well.")

The great, the dominant, the all-controlling fact of this life is commitment. And the task she bequeaths to us, in and through this celebration, is the continuing quest for a new vision, a new aesthetic, a new paradigm which restores art to its true greatness and makes the beautiful a participant and a codefendant of the real and the true and the free. Not art for art's sake nor art for propaganda's sake—Gwendolyn Brooks transcends that false and dangerous and Eurocentric dichotomy, and she calls us to the banner of the "black and unknown bards" of Africa and slavery, who said that art was for life's sake and freedom's sake.

W.E.B. Du Bois said once that "art is not simply works of art; it is the Spirit that knows Beauty, that has music in its soul and the color of sunsets in its hankerchiefs; that can dance on a flaming world and make the world dance, too. Such is the soul of the Negro."

And such is the soul of Gwendolyn Brooks.

She wrote a poem once about a woman boiling an egg. "Being you," she wrote, "you cut your poetry from wood. The boiling of an egg is heavy art. You come upon it as an artist should, with rich-eyed passion, and with straining heart."

One could—and should—say that about Gwendolyn Brooks. Her life is heavy art. Being Gwendolyn Brooks, she cuts her poetry from wood and stone and black steel.

*To Gwen With Love

A Mother's Poem

Haki R. Madhubuti

>   *for G.B.*

not often do we talk
>   destruction was to be mine at 28
>   a bullet in the head or
>   wrong handed lies that would lock
>   me in pale cells that are designed to
>   cut breathing and will
you gave me maturity at daybreak
slashed my heart
and slowed the sprint toward extinction,
delayed my taking on the world alone,
you made living a laborious & loving commitment.

you shared new blood,
challenged mistaken vision,
suggested frequent smiles,
while enlarging life to more than
daily confrontations and lost battles
fought by unprepared poets.

not often did we talk.
your large acts of kindness shaped memory,
your caring penetrated bone & blood
and permanently sculptured a descendant.
i speak of you in smiles
and seldom miss a moment
to thank you for
saving a son.

Thinking On Gwendolyn
Abena Joan Brown

In those quiet, often perplexed moments when I am trying to get to the heart of my own energies and commitments and wondering why, I think on Gwendolyn Brooks. She, along with so many of her kind—the quiet, strong, stalwart ones—has made a profound impact on my consciousness; the rockbed of my deeds.

I don't remember exactly when it started, but this deep admiration of Gwendolyn came to fore in the late sixties. It blossomed to its fullness when I read the tribute, *To Gwendolyn, With Love*. Fortunately, in the schools I attended, Gwendolyn's work was at the core of our literature classes. In that, I was most fortunate. When we met, I remember being stunned that a woman so brilliant could, at the same time, be so modest and unassuming. Her graciousness became apparent when, as Chairperson of a committee to celebrate Paul Robeson's birthday as a community event, I called to ask her to write a poem in commemoration. With laughter in her voice, she asked, "Just like that?"—to which I responded, in my presumptuousness and faith, "Yes, just like that." She wrote the poem, another classic—a clarion call—and I felt honored that she responded so graciously to "little ole me."

As the years went by, Gwendolyn and I interacted around a variety of mutual interests that included young people, Africa, Black people—in general and involving theatre. Gwendolyn Brooks, who seems indefatigable in the breathe and scope of her commitments, nevertheless, always took time to write notes of

16

encouragement as I embarked on stablishing a cultural arts institution for the South Side of Chicago. Her notes came "out of the blue," but always at *that* moment when warmth and support from a person who embodies African values was most needed. I hope my notes have had the same effect for one who so clearly believes as I do in the regenerative properties of reciprocity.

Thinking on Gwendolyn, I realize that I love her very much. Not only for what she represents in talent and basic humanity, but because she embodies that which we have been, what we are and what we can be. Gwendolyn is and because she is, I know that I am.

As Woman   *Walter Bradford*
for Gwendolyn Brooks

I place you in my heart
Solid and perpetual as the March it makes

I am your soldier
Your entire Army.

You launch my dreams others rule incomparable
pull from the shadows all my anxious secrets
turn them gifts the world sings back to me

By and by the sonic dust
records my past bleeps my Vision
to a retreating flash of silver

Work, worry and advanced civilization
Send me, ties my Virtue in syllogism
and I need a song, to lift my trudging heart.

Come, my epic love
speak in single voice
bring heat, and dreams and sermons
to heal and revive
my thirsting blood and dance
Completely.

Gwendolyn Brooks
Angela Jackson

In high school I first saw Gwendolyn Brooks. She was the subject of a short film that one of the nuns showed us in class. That is the way I remember it: a dark, pensive, familiarly pretty woman talking about her life as a writer, or being talked about as a writer. I don't remember which way it was. I remember, however, the first glimpse of her face, and the connection of that face to writing. Memory, I am sure, has mythologized the moment. A truth comes out of the mythology: in beholding her African-dark woman face I saw a premonition of my own. My muse opened the door to Gwendolyn Brooks and kept her seated in my subsconscious.

I am always discovering Gwendolyn Brooks. The young are such arrogant explorers! Europeans to this day believe they discovered Africa. Gwendolyn Brooks, like Africa, has *always* been there. Primary. Evocative. And Inventive. (So often I find myself learning her language.)

I discovered her as a brief memory from girlhood. I discovered her again in 1968 while I was a student in Margaret Walker's Afro-American Literature class at Northwestern. (To go away from home and find your way back, isn't that the journey?) Finally, in those days I discovered her in 1969 shortly after Hoyt W. Fuller invited me to the OBAC Writers Workshop. I discovered everyone who had given birth to me, and given me my birthrite as a writer, a Black writer, an African-American who could be a writer. And Gwendolyn Brooks gave me birthrite as a dark woman writer. Birthrite, duty and privilege. And a profoundly satisfying and self-evoking joy for which my incipient self yearned.

This OBAC-inspired discovery continued. Whatsoever I need know about the technique, the elegance, the vigorous attendance to language in the scrupulous and loving depiction of my life, and life of African America, I plumbed from the work of Gwendolyn Brooks. She made the lessons of the Moderns meaningful. That is the simple truth. I wore out *In the Mecca*, my particular literary Bible. I studied every piece of the geography of *The World of Gwendolyn Brooks*; it helped me give shape to my own landscape. *Maud Martha*, my slim and stunning neighbor, I cherished with the understanding that this faithful regard of her "drylongso" life was a study in the shared humanity and magnificence of Black women, and consequently loving appendix to the lives of a Vast Extraordinary that's made up of Everybody.

Lately, as a college instructor, I discovered Gwendolyn Brooks again, while teaching a course in African-American Women Writers. This discovery, literally, made me tremble. I penned Gwen Brooks a note of gratitude. You see, I discovered that all the giant forces marshalled against the validation of the lives of the Black, the poor, the female, the tender, the foibled and the glorious, Gwendolyn Brooks addressed with shrewd dispatch, clarity, and impeccable beauty and honesty.

Because I now know the terror and difficulty of living the life of the writer, I now know how brave Gwendolyn Brooks is to have nurtured her own gift in a hostile or indifferent environment. I cannot imagine imagining myself as a writer without her (and other!) presanctifying body of work, her presiding and presaging generosity. Without a Gwendolyn Brooks, how did Gwendolyn Brooks dream of herself on this young and ignorant American landscape? I know she must have marshalled every ghost and kinswoman to assist: Phillis Wheatley, Alice Dunbar Nelson, Frances Watkins Harper, Zora Neale Hurston. And a thousand kinsmen. Still, *daring* is a word. *Brilliance* is another.

Discoveries overlap and continue: a writer can give birth to another writer of different strength and disposition. A writer can be a mother. Two equal and demanding roles. A writer can befriend other writers: we need not knock each other down, or stab each other in the back like ravenous careerists. A writer can hold out a hand. Or even open arms to full embrace without diminishing the Self. I can hear her now: a rich, charged Voice denying its influence in my voice when I can document the gifts she's given me. Her genuine humility is a discovery. Her genuine generosity. Her genuine vitality. Her genuine integrity. Her genuine sense of humor. (Any serious writer must have one.) Her genuine bravery.

I am bound to keep on discovering Gwen. (That is what she prefers to be called. In my mind she is Miss Brooks. Just as Hoyt Fuller remains eternally my Mr. Fuller. This is my way of keeping my mythology honest. Miss Brooks. Gwen.) I like and respect the territory. Love is a word. Gratitude is another.

Red Beans and Rice Lady   *Randson C. Boykin*

*Reflections upon visiting the home of Gwendolyn
Brooks, writers workshop, June, 1968.*

something was simple
something was silent and soft
and certainly sensuous
    in a casual way:

the red beans and rice lady
    in her lair the kitchen
fixin food and poetry
    to serve her guests:

we, young writers of
the catharic scream;
the frenzied scheme
of language and life
    bellowing out of our veins

                                    strains
the mind to remember
those days of tortured tales
    and metholed mentionings

the red beans and rice lady
sets out a spread
    of her magic and
mystical prose; invites us
    to eat, and drink, and to recite
our poetry

we are in this special sanctuary
of muses, red beans and rice
and a lady.

With Love To A Friend
Sisi Donald Mosby

More than a few seasons ago a young would-be writer met a very giving and loving person, one who was soaring high above the clouds in the very same stratosphere he longed to enter.

I don't remember when I first decided I was a writer, suffice to say it came very early. I wrote my first news article, a five paragraph sports story, no byline, for the old *Chicago Bee* in 1942. I was a short-never-to-grow-much-taller twelve year old, and I was given free papers to sell, which is how I was paid.

That article, now some 45 years old, resurfaced after years of loving care and safety in the hands of my mother upon her death. It was yellowed and aged, but I still viewed it with wonder.

Not too long after my debut in the *Bee*, the would-be writer was in regular attendance, as a young college student, at the cultural feast which was erupting daily at the Southside Community Art Center.

My purpose for being there was two-fold. There was a writing workshop, and Gwendolyn Brooks was working at the center.

The world was starting all over again. The ravages of World War II were quickly being forgotten, as well as the sacrifice which Black America and black servicemen made helping save the world for democracy.

It was precisely at this point that *A Street In Bronzeville* smashed into my consciousness and snatched me back to reality. It was a rude awakening for a child of the urban ghetto who had never really examined the world surrounding him.

At the same time I was twice blessed because Gwendolyn Brooks became my lifelong friend. In future years she would welcome me in her home, several of them, and graciously share the hard won skills and wisdom she carried within her.

She became *the* standard by which I judged myself. I know now I was blessed because, thanks to Gwen, I never had to undergo the painful self-searching many black writers endured, after being weaned on the great white writers of Western literature.

I stopped reading most white writers long ago because I could not relate to what they said. This is not to say I do not appreciate

22

their talent. But because Gwendolyn Brooks was my first, and only, literary hero, I remained firmly rooted in black culture.

It was, and is, a precious gift.

Upon deciding I was a writer I devoured the artsy literary review magazines. I quickly discovered there was very little in them about black writers. After reading *A Street In Bronzeville* I understood the sense of apartness I felt when I read the reviews. I realized I was an outsider peeping through the window.

In *A Street In Bronzeville* everything was in sharp focus. It was about me. I lived there, I walked those streets, and I knew the people about whom Gwen wrote.

It was like being born again!

How does one pay a fitting tribute to his own personal hero?

Thank you kind friend, I am forever grateful.

For Gwen Brooks   *Zack Gilbert*

On Her Seventh Birthday

You paint life
Pictures with words.
Build your castles
Of truth dreams
With bricks of steel.
And as our days
Move into the eternity
Of time.
Bombarded by thunder
And slashed by the quick
Whips of lightning.
Your creations survive.
A rainbow
After the death storm;
Life seeds in
The womb of the mind.

The Way Back Home
Sandra Jackson-Opoku

When I was a little girl I used to get lost a lot. If I ventured more than a few blocks from home, I was bound to have trouble finding my way back.

I remember starting a new school in the sixth grade. Let out at lunchtime by a different door than the one I came in, I was utterly disoriented. I wandered routeless, trying to find my way home for lunch. It was fruitless. I finally made my way back to school and continued the day on an empty stomach.

Well, I still get lost. My internal compass veers off when driving those diagonal streets of Chicago, old Indian trails that wander of the straight and narrow grids of carefully numbered drives and avenues. But I've learned to compensate. To memorize landmarks that I follow that always lead me back home.

There are times when a Black woman writer feels alone in the world. Rootless, routeless. Lost and wandering. But there is a landmark in these streetscapes of open wounds and broken words. A lighthouse whose beacon always illuminates the way back home. Or a brook, a singing silver thread lacing this black earth. This body of water bubbles up from deep and secret origins. It sparkles with quenching waters. And a voice echoes with ages. She has always been there. She will always be.

Miss Gwendolyn Brooks is that literary landmark, that lighthouse. That winding, quenching way of water.

Brooks' poetry celebrates the ordinary wonderfulness of Black life. It silhouettes the minute acts of heroism that make men and women immortal. Her poetry is food; it nourishes the spirit. It is water; it renews the soul.

Reading Gwendolyn Brooks' work is a ritual act of rejuvenation and enrichment. It is like walking out of your house and finding jewels scattered amongst the weeds and grass.

One does not like to play favorites with masterpieces. It seems like choosing a favorite child. Each gem sparkles in different multi-facets. But the one I keep coming back to, that I know as I know my mother's smile, is "For Sisters Who Have Kept Their Naturals."

It glistens and shines as does Brooks' own glorious crown, earth black and laced with silver. It resonates like a singing brook. And in a world that struggles to stretch and straighten out the secret curls and coils of our Black lives, it shimmers like a lighthouse. *She* shimmers like a lighthouse.

Illuminating the way back home.

She   *Ginger Mance*

for Gwendolyn Brooks

She
wakes spirits within us
old and young
calls forth
the yet to come
makes us jazz
makes us blues
makes us rhythm
makes us move
She
speaks to us
in song
in season
speaks to us
in reason

She

A Singular Woman
Beryl Zitch

It was 1967 when I received a short note: "Can't we be Gwen and Beryl, since we'll be working together?" That certainly wasn't my first clue to the generosity and caring of Gwendolyn Brooks, but I've kept that note all this time since it was the beginning of a relationship I've cherished for over 20 years—a reminder of her thoughtfulness, grace and just 'niceness.'

Over those years we've shared many highs and lows. Family losses seemed to happen to us both at the same time and so we've shared tears as well.

70 years?—I can't believe it! She moves with the energy of the whirlwind she writes about so vividly. She reads her poetry with all the elan, vibrancy, drama and excitement of a new poet enthusiastically trying to make his/her way. Constantly renewing her vision, to see with original freshness what stands before her, what she sees are symbols of regeneration. What her audiences and readers receive from her is commitment, honesty, empathy and dedication. She is a mind-challenger, encouraging young people to look at the world around them differently ever after, and generously recognizing burgeoning and established writers in her numerous awards.

And after all these more than 20 years, I am still fascinated by her wonder and facility—still somewhat in awe—and *still* unable to imagine what life would have been had I not had the opportunity to know, love, admire and respect this singular woman. Gwendolyn Brooks, I applaud you!

Mother *Sterling D. Plumpp*

for Gwendolyn Brooks

It
would be
any
way. The song
that held
my mother.

26

As
she ripped
sky to make
a pallet.
For
my crossing in
to tones. That
song would
be.
would
get up
holding on
to ragged edges
patched by weeping
clouds. That
song
would be
any
way. Be
cause
my mother
hid
it
in honky
tonk rhythms of:
I will
work on
you. I reached
from the hybrid
of my blues and
found
it.
Distilled
in chocolates
of your wombing lines.
To self.

A Whole And Beautiful Spirit

Johari Amini

for Gwendolyn Brooks
"...an act of living is an act
of love..."—David Llorens

in the beginning was the sight
of blackness & was the seed
a sight which lives an act of love
a cite of images/creation of
where we must go & where we must be
(& also why
(listen to her eyes as they see us
a sight of poems blackpoems
peoplepoems poems for directions/finders
site movers moving image values
moving to cite beauty moving to
proclaim love & other holy things
(& sight reflections of poet/being
written & spoken & heard from cite seed
vibrations which are
(for she is a sure direction/voice
(which makes us brittle in ourselves
moving selfhate moving dross
changing moving toward the cite
of blackness beginning from the seed
beginning from her sight which is
an act of love which is an act of
life

Afrikan Woman

Useni Eugene Perkins

for Gwendolyn Brooks

if I were to build
a monument for you
I would search for Afrikan soil
and mix it with unjaded water
from the ancient River Niger

then I would go to
the crest for the Nile Valley
and let the substance
repose under the equatorial sun
until it has absorbed
the history of our ancestors

I would then begin to shape
the contour of your face
from the image of Queen Neferteri
and take it to Nigeria
so the Yoruba Gods
could bless your fertility
with the fragrance of
incense and natural perfumes
from the legacy of Queen Yaa Asantewa
and carve your deeds
from the charisma of Queen Nzingha

the I would take your body
at the top of Mt. Kilimajaro
and let the cool wind
blow against your ebony flesh
and after you had felt
the breeze of nature's rapture
I would caress your body
and lay it among
the verdant trees of Kenya

until life became woman
and woman became life

until the praise songs
of the Ashanti, Ibo and Zulu
were heard from
the shores of Malagasy
to the red sands of the Sudan
from the tip of the Ivory Coast
to the Great Riff Valley in Mozambique

until the butterflies of Tanzania
spread their beautiful colors
throughout Swaziland and Azania
until the drums of Juba
and the drums of Chaga

and the drums of Shango
sound ju ju chants
to our Afrikan ancestors

and your elegant body
would be placed in ebony gold
for the world to admire
and for Black men to behold

and your monumenmt
would be complete
a definitive statement
of Afrikan Womanhood

From the Diaspora: Poets

Sterling Brown and Gwendolyn

Roy Lewis

Gwendolyn Brooks at Temple University

Sonia Sanchez

how to write of this pulitzer prize woman
whose coming reminds us of cloisters of black marble?
how to celebrate this poet laureate woman whose
ellingtonian nocturnes saturate us with
jewels and magic? how to introduce this
woman of lace and fire whose words ride
bareback on our tongues delivering memories?
i guess. i'll say sistergwen. friend. comrade.
guardian of mornings.
                    woman. whose color of life is
like the sun. whose laughter is prayer.

For Gwen, My Mentor, My Friend   *Jeanette Adams*

    Gwendolyn Elizabeth Brooks:
gentle
generous
word-woman
daughter of Isis

lovely as a pikani lei
rare bloom citrus scent
provocative as a black sand beach
volcanic
vital

    Gwendolyn Elizabeth Brooks:
dreamer
discoverer
word-woman
daughter of Isis
herstoric heroine
necessary nourishment

Mother Tongue   *Fatimah Afif*

    for Gwen Brooks

MotherTongue
    Tongue
    Tongue

We celebrate you inArabic
        Wolof
        Yoruba
        Kikuyu
          and

Offer our words as libations to Candice, Nzinga, and Hatsheput
The High Priestesses of our Destiny

We anoint the air, like frankincense, with tales of
Harriet, Rosa, and Assata
Who preceded us through your Rites of Passage

In this ceremony of verse,
We dance, sing, and swing our poems
Loosely around our hips like a konga of kente
Inticing the drum to beat your rhythms, Mother Tongue

Voice of a thousand seasons
Poet of the Rain Forests
Dogon-Spirit Woman

Your Life is a ritual we perform.

Gwendolyn Was Here/Is   *Estella Conwill Alexander*

> *...have your blooming*
> *in the noise of the whirlwind.*"

at each blooming
a scarification—

an empowered etching
as if upon a hard slab
    of wind—

her search
scraps urgently
against the awesome swirl
creating a lithography of words
upon our soul—
evoking memory
and vision
and new geography of being—

serious symbols
saying at once
gwendolyn was here/is—
a whole culture
can make a passage
through her passages
impressed
and owned
only in purest moments
before the liquid dries
upon the stone—

gwendolyn is here—
is indeliably here
empowering culture—
claiming life.

The Call/Response   *Estella Conwill Alexander*

for Gwendolyn Brooks

Who will let me hear my own voice
in deep dark woman tones?
be my black and stone believer?
who will make my meccas known?
who will mirror my holy essense—
shatter the sufferer's moan—
gather gut and marrow gladness
to make some magic of your own
to transform flesh into words—
to speak the vision—make them see
their bonding magnifying
into whole fragments of me?

Gwendolyn Brooks   *Fareedah Allah*

She came to the Nation's Capitol, the citadel of the Nation's culture;
she came crowned Poet Laureate, America's.

She walked among the dead letters, the dead language, the dead scholars
of the Library of Congress carrying life and the warmth of Love for
everyone. She walked humbly.

She pushed open the heavy redwood doors of racism.
She forced up the federal security, storm windows of rejections
allowing the fresh breeze of a new world poetry to filter into the
musty halls, disturbing the dust, and moving the hearts of America.

She invited Haki Madhubuti, Sonia Sanchez, Mari Evans, and James Baldwin
to walk proudly onto the stage of the Great Hall, to stand before a standing
ovation/audience and read...read a long ignored American literature, a new
world poetry, life blood for a dying culture.

She came walking softly, smiling kindly, in a humble manner, talking, answering letters from unknown poets.

She came to the Nation's Capitol, the Citadel of the Nation's culture, she came crowned Poet Laureate, America's.

The Griot We Know
Molefi Asante

Griot immortal!
water spirit from dancing
twinness from the sky
eloquent sage of our youth
and termite mounds
listening for Amma's replay
with feet on the ground

Nommo of eightness
bright light of black sun
shines luminous in bound
against the gray
lighting shrines to ancestors
as voices of Gwendolyn
rise higher in this day.

Gwendolyn Brooks: A Rediscovery
William Beyer

Rereading your celebrated *Annie Allen*
after twenty-five years.
I find the same surge
of sudden joy,
depths of grief
carefully mingled together;
a subtle blend.

I visualize,
experience again
the immediate world
that was your own,
closed in by fences of prejudice,
intense anger,
a lingering mood of desperation;
surrounding violence
within the ghetto streets.

Your poet-passions
still excite.
are intricately woven
in the words;
changing emotional colors
of your perfectly crafted lines.

Dennis Brutus

for Gwendolyn Brooks

still the indifferent waves
wash the shores of West Africa

still they hurl themselves
with imagined fury
against the crumbling landspits

still they shatter
into sundered fragments

on the stoic shoulders
of the blade-edge rocks

and still they draw back
and gather their energies
heaving to a menacing surge
and move with a deep throaty roar
for one fresh tireless assault.

On First Meeting   *Barbara Cochran*

Like pooled resources
we gathered at the open
hearth.

On a cold day, in 1973
we gathered to see
a poet laureate.

Would-be writers clutching
small parcels, like
uncovered treasures

And feeling proud
cause she was black
and poet laureate.

On a small college
campus, in Lake Forest
we gathered near the
open fire—
the poet laureate,
watched the
knowing eyes.

And we listened as
she talked of poetry
and it's common thread . . .
life

She opened her warmth
to young people and
those still impressed
with moons.

And the poet laureate
left a bit of sun, on
a cold day, in 1973

Dinner With the Poet
at Plattsburgh

Linda Cousins

to Gwendolyn Brooks

an unassuming fare
for her:

roast duck—crisply crisp
patiently awaited
                no salad
                no hors d'ouevres
                no alcohol
                (not even the pretty pink
                daiquiri
                with whisps of whipped cream
                and a courageous cherry
                perched precariously atop)

the elegant restaurant
overlooking a placid
          Plattsburgh river
a dinner in honor
     of the peaceful poet
          of gentle power
the pretentious-less Poet
          of persistent, prodding
                         presence—
                         quite positive

al illustrious company
in her honor here
yet the peaceful poet
          of gentle power
speaks not erudition
but wayshowing words
          of edifying elder-encouragement
to the shy golden children
across the table
               to the bright young boy
               with long-lashed downcast
               eyes
               and to the small girl
               who reveals that she creatively
                  savors short stories
                     in her soul

the children
taste the sweetness
of a poet/Spirit
at this dinner table
in Plattsburgh
and smile love

their young eyes
film
nourishing memories
to grow and travel
with them
through their to-be
     years.

she radiates
a Life and a love
a living
and a loving
    that particular way
this poet
      in Plattsburgh
for a Black Poetry Day

amtrak-arrived
a mother-poet
        of our poets
a decades-daughter here

yet for her
an unassuming fare:

roast duck—crisply crisp

      no salad
      no alcohol
just the children
      here
and a peaceful river
      over there

and the elder Poet
      of our poets
      the mother-Poet
      of our poets
for Black Poetry Day
    in Plattsburgh.

Diluted Negroe *Dawn R. Crump*

After reading "The Life of Lincoln West"

Always
in the middle, middle,
the yellow middle
the middle class middle
the middle where
almost white hatred
keeps you in the black hole
dark folding sun sucking
all the light into the gut hole
of no place you belong
middle.

The middle
the fence
the indecision
the embodiment of who
you become not
middle.

Where covetous cloaked
in red spreads its tongue
to promise you acceptance
and no more misfit, misplaced,
wedged between the wall of two
asses shitting on you and you out
middle.

The middle
the rope swinging
body dangling
between limb and dirt
middle
the hate
the boredom
the angry
middle
where balanced words
are spoken

gray
mulatto
human words
that try to
say I look comfortable
where I am
but the walls of your
ass squeeze me 'til I bleed
middle.

Real thing -
you have a place to stand. A rock of accusation
to splash my mingled blood
on and watch it creep thick
with no place to go

like a slow man defending
his woman at gunpoint
middle.

A Sahel Mother

Bibhas R. De

> *On any hill or plain or crawling cot*
> *Or gentle for the lilyless hasty pall*
> *—Gwendolyn Brooks*

Was it written then
That laid bare by the wayside
Her life's prime was to play out
In this grim footlight parade
Screened across the seas
Six o'clock nightly at suppertime,
Her tattered shreds denying privacy,
A stack of bones wrapped in skin?
Love she had known once, fulfilling
Her new found desires, bringing
Blessings of earth upon her womb;
And now the shriveled little mouth
Tugs weakly at her milkless teats
In this marred temple of her youth
As both perish of a bitter winter
In a nest never woven.

Earth, honor her great dignity
Hold up her lamp for eternity.

The Stillness

Rutt Dennis

for Gwendolyn Brooks

They say
still waters
run deep.
well you're
the stillest
and
the deepest.
so still
that your quietness
evokes fear
among the brain-smashers
whose minds
are on permanent leave
in corporate paradise.
   so deep
that your words fall
on bubbly faces
which gush
and remain
blind and deaf
to the truth-bombs
you release
with the gentle tilt
of your head.
weave your stories
of life
and love
of hopes
and fears
and explain
our yesterdays
so that our tomorrows
shine
with new light.
help our stillness
to resound
like a million
suns in collusion
and our deepness
to be rooted

in the wisdom
of the ancient sages.
you're still
and deep
and your words
are magical
in a world
that has sought
to exile reality toi
Wall Street

Thinking of Gwendolyn Brooks
On the Occasion of Her Sevenieth Birthday

Sherman L. Fowler

Cerebral nerve endings
Connect and conjure
This hallowed image:
Sparkling Afro-American Nightingale,
Sagacious griot-songstress—Sprung
Graciously from the fertile
Glands of Archaic River-Niger.
YEMOJIC whistler of
Divine themes and
Flowering dreams—melodic
Whistler, Fluting life's
Cherished Poem-Songs:
Insights for all TIME!

Now There Should Be Roses

R. Nyatau Glasco

First there were smells of security
fertile lands,
kingdom of even-cut shrubs
your front yard.
You hid behind picket fences
staring at a
blemished, corrupt, curious world.
You had not earned it.
It had been given.
You climbed the fence
stood in alleyways
embracing charity's children.
And now there should be roses
Sun turned, dew kissed roses

With pen in hand
you sliced open
peeled back our flesh.
Through syllables and sounds
you revealed societal ills.
And now there should be roses
Fiill bloomed, teacher apple-red roses
for ONE who has fought and taught,
fought and taught
US
H U M A N I T A R I A N I S M

For Gwen, With Love   *Vivian Verdell Gordon*

In those times
when I SPIN around
Shakingly, Whirlingly, Otherworldly,
when I loose boundaries
of sky and ground
when I think myself upside down
directionless
undefined

I pull wisdom from my shelf
and read:
    Sisters
    ...
    prevail
    prevail across the editors
    of the world!
    ...
    there have been trampelings
    ...
    And you create and train
    your flowers still.

Then,
I walk erect
into the world.

Ode to Gwendolyn Brooks

Sharon Leonard Goodman

Her animated voice
Speaks of old loves
Through bespeckled half-moon eyes

Lips paused and perched
Open wide and smile out proud
Tall African warriors or
The soul of Black folks just
Too tired to live

She is a survivor who
Has managed to survive
So many it/ain't/gonna/be/easy days
Gwen nourishes an unconquerable spirit
That has risen from the depths of pyramids
And propelled beyond life itself

Gwendolyn
I mean Gwendolyn is so full of herself
She soars past her own ego
Poeting joy and pain
Of our Blackness
Of our people

For Gwen Brooks on her Sevenieth Birthday

Stephen E. Henderson

Praise God
Sing Hallelujah
For Gwendolyn Brooks
Ancestral grace
Boo-coos of bouquets
For you Gwen
Agile explorer of the spirit side
Of the underside of life

Sing hallelujah
Ancestral grace
For "the daylight" of *your* wisdom
For the tensile strength
Of your soul
For your largesse
Your "gobbling mother-eye"
For your caring, Gwen,
For your love

A Song You Have The Music To

Fred L. Hord

I lifted this song with your books,
read them all again,
shared your love
of saying your love
while you lived it even better.

I looked for your alliterate lovelies
that were too happy to stand alone,
soft black bridal gowns
lacing the one best dark suit.

But I could not wed them as wisely
as your joining,
nor alter new pairs
for lasting ceremony.

And so I returned to the Howard chapel
that you filled with musical prayer
to offer broken rhythms to the sure cadences
of your life and lyric.

Each day I teach Lincoln in the West
and chocolate Mabbie dreaming marble.
Lincoln wants to be president
and Mabbie sits on her hair in the front yard.

We need you here at Howard.
We need the mirrors of your love lessons,
the clean polished glass of your mothering
to show our lives free alliteration.

We need the miracle of your metamorphosis,
the golden choice to pat your fleece,
to jet the double fleecers of your day,
giving us starred night in which to believe.

Broadside was better for your ballista,
and Third World the best way for developing
rich land we thought was arid,
just with the power of your singing.

Sing on, Miss Brooks,
with your spring spirit greening us.
Marry us with your wisdom,
with the music of your trust.

I sang with you once, Miss Brooks,
on the banks of a Wabash you made black,
with Haki, a tall son sunning us,
we three lyricing wind at the students' back.

This song is a memorial to a Topeka girl,
whose decisions were both black and supreme.
In the forever that is left of your life,
keep us awake with your sonorous dreams.

Amelia Blossom House

Gwendolyn—lady of new vision
I have heard
your voice
clear
rising at the dawning
sings the lark
sings the lark
Mother of poets
I have seen
your fearless protection
of the young
jealouslyi guarding
their fragile futures
nurturing new voices
to rise against the noon sky
sings the lark, sings the lark
First lady of your visions
you have taught
our souls to sing
freedom
against the setting sun
sings the lark.

Gwendolyn Brooks   *Kathleen M. Kemmerer*

A melifluous, bucolic name
From which no pastorals issue
A city-centered poet
Whose clarity of vision
Crystalizes hard black reality
Into fine diamonds.

Poem for the Black Woman   *Shirley Bradley LeFlore*

Dedicated to Gwendolyn Brooks

i house the legend of mutima
i am the heartbeat of the earth
the offspring of the moon and the sun
thrust from the energy of afrika
i am the black woman
the symbol of love
the channel of creation
the vibration of peace
the anger of storms
the pain of suffering
i am the black woman
i have seen the first rain
and the last fire.
i am seasoner of soul
many tales untold
i am the black woman
my womb stretches across the mouth of the universe
to create rhythms and nations
my body has borne witness to birth
my spirit, the taster of death
i have seen the 13th month
and the 32nd day
the year 3000 before the year 03
i am the black woman
i have cradled the newborn's cry
and the ole-man's moan
and rocked the smiles of aging
nature in my arms
i am the other part of god
i am the other side of man
i am the spirit of life
i am the black woman.

Gwendolyn Reading
In Black Voice

Robert Lima

"Ugly" is had enough as it is,
but she stretched it out in black
deep in her gut and
brought it to the surface,
making it rise up in throatiness:
ü ü ü g´ l i

And the little boy in the poem
came alive through the sympathy
of her deep black voice
belching the ugliness he felt
when Black is supposed to be
b ü´ t i f o o H

For Gwen

Naomi Long Madgett

Your are our gardener in a land of blight.
You enrich arid soil, purify
polluted air, shower on us benedictions
of sun and rain.

Because of your hands' gentleness,
fragile stalks grow strong,
healthy roots burrow deep
expanding their power.

Strengthened by your spirit,
nurtured by your caring,
we blossom for you, dear sister.
We give you our sunflower faces
as a token of our love.

We Remember You Well

Thad Mathis

We remember you well, gentle lady.
Your images cut, and sear
And burn and tear
and slowly wind their way
Along the narrow crevices of
Carefully tucked away yesterdays;
And move us.

We squire, your revelations come so near;
Sometimes we fear, your words strip us naked.
We exhault with swollen tear
Your velvet warmth and wit,
Your little Lincoln West and the Sundays of Satin Legs Smith.

Your words in gala garb, walk proudly
Through the cobwebbed corridors of our consciousness.
Pristine. Pausing long enough to wink,
Like perky two-year olds.
The echoes of your craft—like bashful lovers -
Hum sweet nothings in our ear. Softly.
Sometimes imperceptibly
Always well.

Black Enough

Thad Mathis

Bold. Black. Beautiful
You are, sweet Gwen. The power Of your craft transforms.

Two Poems For Gwendolyn Brooks

D.H. Melhem

1.

A matter of poetry and power: the power of
poetry raised to the rhetoric of
music, an orchestration
by cultural strings, chords
of drums and chanting
toward harmony or dissonance
a syncopation of
rage and rejoicing
an architecture
familial

Gwen:

  the strength is love
  soled and sewn, the
  underside of anger like
  sun, its ray sustaining
  the eye
  lifting to the
  face of a child
  with its day ahead
  power to you: Gwen

2.

Jewel-cutters may wound us
with tools, facet edges
mayi scratch, weight and
sparkle will be fine to
the eye, yet in the touch,
                              cool.

You
give jewels
and your hand
goes with the giving,
revives the rock.

The Other   *Gwendolyn Mitchell*

She was words before words,
     this long glassed
          angled brown poet woman.
Her visions challenged beyond street seen
     making whole
          the fragment of "Bronzeville"
               and so much familiar.
Her poems
     untimed and thick of flesh,
          and quiet
               steadied many a
                    young struggle.
Fresh truths
     were loud upon ths
          sunned tongue.
Her noise is of blooming
     this whirlwind
          coming.

In Essence   *dorothea m. moore*

          In Honor of Gwendolyn Brooks

generating ethos
from heart
felt meanings
looking deep
into the expressions
of time

past a street
on Bronzeville
sweet smell of
the magnolias
blooming in Faith
her willingness.
courage to look
underneath and
expose the
true meaning
Noble
The Kuumba
speaking loudly
sweetly from
the soul of
her inner self
awakens the
ears of the
dreamers sleep

open up hear
what words
are imparting
opening up
the arts
within the
beings of
rivers runnig
within

Lenard D. Moore

Dear Gwendolyn Brooks
I come from a black ground
that hungers for salvation
calling through darkness
like an owl

I come from a black ground
that have visions of purification
dreaming against bitterness
like our ancestors

I come from a black ground
that echoes through thick air
wanting a wordless poem
like you, Gwen

To Gwen, Painter of Words

Maria K. Mootry

Priestess, portraitess, painter of words,
You caught us in all our postures:
The costumes, cosmetics and shifting architecture of our days
    Across your unfolding canvas marched
Chocolate Mabbie & Pearl May Lee, Annie Allen & Big Bessie:
Lester, Pee Wee, Satin-Legs & Alfred, the poet warrior.
All those moments of ennui, of confusion, of pain, of defiance.
The black and tan and yellow of it.
You liked the crush, the concentration of words (you said)
As painters love tempura's varied textures, water color's
    transparency, the opacity of oils.
And you did it.
You fixed us, at once inside and outside History,
Our images frozen in protean patterns
Forever negotiating between imagination and reality.
A lilting, luminescent, longlived legacy.
The signature, your brushwork words.

April Foolin' Around

Akua Serwaa Omowale

for Gwendolyn Brooks, Happy Solar Return

Gwen Brooks
Lyrically babbling
Miss Real Cool

    Tried to school
    Lot' sa c/old but
    None too bold
        Fools
    Before they cud fall
    Into the caul drone
    of lifeless nomes and
    Mindless moans

(prepared for them by the wicked switch witches)

Yes, we've eaten beans too
When we've really had two
Cents over carfare 'til payday,
Or Like Maria de Jesus
    Used to say
          "The unschooled ate beans
        But not the Brown, the Black
            Were hidden in
              Brazil's favela-ed stacks
Where homeless masses loitered in-sane censored shacks"
        Waiting for society's judgment to comply
        Waiting for resurrection
        Waiting to die

        So the Cat on the Block
        Put his hand to the Clock
            "Tick, tock; tock, tock"
    Just in time to stop SELF-IMPLOSION
           GENETIC EXPLOSION
               Destruction
               Recon-functioned

(headline: MASTERS PLAN GONE AWRY!)

Some Tht in tune
Some Laughed too soon
Others wanted to die
But couldn't find June
   Only the john and that required a key
   "Damn," tht they, "we only wanted to pee!"

So Now
        B(l)ack to schoo
No more an(un) ed-ju-cated fool.

Many need but cannot read/feed
They've survived the pale
Of the slave-boy's jail

So Now
        They seek Walker/Washington/Douglass/DuBois

To See How
>Garvey and Malcolm all made the same choice
>When they said to the masses
>"BOYCOTT GIN and
>Ignorance produced by classes.
>It's a real living sin
>This stoned trek to the grave
>Keep self and yours sacred:

>JOIN OUR SUN-KNOWLEDGE CRAZE."

Baobab
Raymond R. Patterson

>*for Gwendolyn Brooks*

>Tree-Mother
>Sacred Tree Rooted in Sun and Soil
>Tree of the Spirits of Children Waiting To Be Born
>Tree Who Shelters Caravans
>Shade Tree of the Littlest Ones, Who Never Tires of Their Songs
>Tree of White, Pendulous Flowers
>Tree of the Fulness of Night
>Tree-Mother, we thank you
>for your fruit, we thank you
>for your fiber (to weave
>our clothes) we thank you
>for your medicine (to treat
>our ills) we thank you.
>Bees store in your hollows
>the sweetest honey, we thank you.
>Your children thank you, saying your name.
>Teach us the strength of your branch and root.
>Teach us the wisdom of your monumental growing.

In Her Honor
Robert Earl Price

>*for Gwendolyn Brooks)*

This woman of work and wonder
is a righteous rain and a fierce fog.
She toils and dreams in our midst
carries water from many rivers.

This urn of sacred rainbows
a wellspring of voices

a fountainhead of songs
this bubble, this branch, this brook
this prayer, this passion, this poet
this leeward bayou
this liquid logic
pumping love and legend
thru the people's heart.
With ink and insight
she seeds our souls
salts our tears
and speaks our mind.

If we respect our elders
we must embrace her
if we embrace our past
we must value her
if we value courage
we must drink her up
like communion wine.
This life, this love, this legacy
this bilet doux
this breathing book
this Black sea
this Brownstone oracle
this boiling brook.

If we harbor hope
we must shelter her.
If we shelter our prophets
we must pay homage
to this hallowed headwater
this blessed
this beloved
Gwendolyn Brooks.

GwensWays

Eugene B. Redmond

for Gwendolyn Brooks

Cautious & Incantatory,
Proverbial & Incremental,
Kinetic & Incendiary,
    She Languages down
The unilluminated

Avenues
Of The inflated;
The sleepwoke;
The impish; The august; The possessed;
The disengaged; The emblematic; The ugly;
     Wearing her—
make you wanna hiss/make you wanna hush
     —verbal amulets divine
     Like crosses;

Pith
Parchment and
Prophecy
     Fly from this intersperser of Dread-Words;
O, the ways of our
Wise counterclock woman!

          Momenting the Ancestrail:
Evocative, uneclipsed, evangelical:

And
Intricate:
Her Call/Our Response
Continuity.

Hard Rock Gwen   *A. Oliver Shands*

There's a kind of
hard rock
in Gwen Brooks.

There's her
upside-down
smile.

And Gwen herself
takes to a
reading of Etheridge Knight's
Hard Rock
from time to
time.

Gues what else?

I heard her say
something about

not being one
to fancy
wearing
flowers.

And, I know
there had to
be those times
when she just
slammed back
like a hard rock —
or you might
want to say
a diamond.

Have You Met Miss Brooks?

Saundra Sharp

i came breathless to meet her
this grand grandmother
       sensible shoes
duster of family pictures
       strand of pearls
recorder of negroness
       organized papers
mother of annie allen
       touch of gray
knighted lady of prizes
       delicate strength

i came faint to meet her
this farmer of
bean eaters and wordworkers

Mecca was waiting
she real cool
blue jeans
combat boots
red socks
kinked hair
levis lady
leading the word revolution

**An Obelisk in the Valley
  Of the Queens**   *Askia M. Touré*

    In Tribute to Ms. Gwendolyn Brooks

To flourish in a world intimidated
by implications of your
holy vision:
a harmonious chant
to higher dimensions of our
Afrikanity.

O Priestess;
        your very essence, even in
silence, speaks volumes for a World
purged of the Aryan Lie.
A World where our genius
can bloom in grandiose complexity,
sparking milleniums of golden ages
balanced upon the apex
of a Great Pyramid.
In this sanguine age of Holocaust,
when Afrikan lives are less than dung,
yours is the promise soaring
in Robeson's voice: immaculate grandeur
poised against a rabid genocide.
In my regard for your magnificent
Consistency,
        I offer this poem, a tiny ankh
from the Ancestors,
as tribute to your
transcendental love . . .

O Gwen, Queen-mother;
Oracle, Living — Forever!

Our MZ Brooks: Clearing Space at the LOC   *Eleanor Traylor*

The poet
    walking brownly
        subdues
the stage

    Pours
garnet, topaz, borealis,

yemiyaw blue
        sets
onynx stars
        in
golden crowns
        of
triplets. iambs. quadrametic
        song.

Querying. her glance calls loudly.
        yet unperturbed.
"Pepita. Pepita. where is Pepita?
"Pepita. Pepita. where Pepita?
"Pepita. Pepita. where is Pepita?

"Answers "hoodo holler" through
the white washed room
gathering like some gentle
        cloud
raining on the memory
    of our dreams:
Pepita here! Pepita here! Pepita. here is Pepita!
Pepita here! Pepita here! Pepita. hear Pepita.
We are all. Pepita. here.

Wendy, Stand Up With Your Proud Hair

Sandra West

When the daze of this day comes done
These days of dreadlocks
Vs dark 'n lovely goldilocks et al.

Wendy still wears her natural.

Gwendolyn Brooks calls Wendy to her feet
As in"... and I'd like to recognize
Sister-Reverend-Doctor-Bishop-so-and-so..."

The poet's statement of purpose.
The blackest aesthetic.
Never pales from style.

As Gwendolyn speaks
To the gerri curled. california furled
Revlon flexed and hexed girls.

Wendy still wears her natural.

Like the pen of the poet
That speaks the truth plain
Happily, knappily, as it lays.

The Words Remain

Kimmika L.H. Williams

for Gwendolyn Brooks

She's been teaching us,
pushing herself
"working" each day,
recording her path
while time eases
away —
but the words remain!

Going on — still
the pace might slow
growing wearing at days' end;
her eye sight has dimmed
and, no doubt,
the body will bend —
but, the words remain!

Revelation

Alred L. Woods

On the livingroom radio, WVON live broadcast
gospel music from New Zion Baptist Church blast
I sprawled across the kitchen table reading
a poem in the verse section of the Sunday magazine.
In it I discovered what I had to do.

Still in pajamas and Daddy's bath robe
I read a poem that for me marked time.
There was a time before and time after
I ever read poetry by Gwendolyn Brooks,
a time when I enjoyed reading poetry and
a time when writing it was something I could do.

For the first time I discovered something in words
related to me. I heard a music in
Gwendolyn Brooks' poetry that morning,

a music not like that in the Boys' Book of Verse,
not like Dunbar, Yeats, Baraka, and many many others
I later read. I heard a music in her poetry,
a music I read whenever I heard the word mother.

On Your Special Day   *Stephen Caldwell Wright*
         for Gwendolyn Brooks

You are in your circle.
In the crowd.
Not cloistered nor conformed.
No satin.
No corsages.
          (No tuxedos.
          No Bowties.
          Requested.)
No.
In your circle—Divine Divesture.
No question.
Such Flair, Flawless.
          In your circle.
          In the crowd.
Apart.
Still.
Moving and being Moved.
Resiliently Affirmative
Not by Quota.
Religiously Sure.

An Arrangement in the Language of Flowers   *Sander Zulauf*
         for Gwendolyn Brooks

African violet: "Such worth is rare,"
Available, kind, pure.
Camellia: "Reflected loveliness,"
Spring water in Eden.
Chrysanthemums, red and white:
"I love," "Turth,"
Aquifer of soul.
Mint: "Virtue,"
Vigorous evangelist spreading comfort.
Orchid: "Beauty, magnificence"

Gentle pilgrim successfully surviving.
Zinnia: "Thoughts of absent friends."
Brothers and sisters, parents and children,
Thoughts that never think of giving up
The fight for emotional
Justice, holy physical
Freedom, equal harmonious
Peace, watch the wake behind you:
Brooks Jr. High School.
Can you imagine?
The Chicago *Defender*.
The Blackstone Rangers.
Real Cool and
Your
Mama died a few months
After her house was
Invaded, invaded.
She died after she
Was invaded.
Genius (and Orange Blossom,
Lightly orange: "Your purity
Equals your loveliness")
Is no accident, no Lincoln
West oddity, for fearsome
Public display, no sacrosanct
Agility of manipulation,
No false notes. You either have it
(The *real* thing) or
You don't. Evil is omnipresent
But living is the Orange
And Poetry is Life Distilled
And inner revolutions
Far outdistance invasions.
Inner revolutions are where
Differences begin, and there will be
No king-sized bed for you,
Rather one $5 less per night
Would be just fine,
Right for a modest rest
After a long time
On the road and the railroad
(For the only places you regularly
Soar are on paper and
Into the face of oppression)
A rest few so blessed

Acquire, who share light simply
And balance it perfectly,
Delicate with the dark for a while
Then move on. Sneakers
Squeak in gyms, and basketball
Was made for city kids.
One on one, until the last
Is satisfactorily answered.
As Laureate, a good poem for the Mayor,
Making Chicago welcome him
Completely on the day
He welcomed Chicago into his veins.
Dear Gwendolyn,
As you grow older
Ever so slightly
And eat less meat
and drink less hot coffee
Sudden flowers from the train window
Greet you, say their soft prayers
For you as you pass
And make your way
Cross country.

The Woman, The Work, The Music

Gwendolyn and Students

For Gwen: A Praisesong
Eugenia Collier

Spirit-mother,
conjurer of miracles,
mythmaker, joy-giver,
singer of Life, cajoling us
from ashes to air—
how can I sing your praise?

O Gwen! I sit here clutching my pen, gazing at the oak outside my window, whose complex patterns usually coax from me the reluctant words, and I wait—but nothing comes.

Because there is too much. Because the poet in me wants to sing you a praisesong, the critic in me wants to proclaim the infinite value of your work, the tale-teller in me wants to narrate the story of your travail and triumph. And so I gaze at my oak and the two maples behind it. The boughs swaying languidly, the new spring leaves, the morning sunlight filtering through—all, all carol Life.

And now the dissonant voices within me emerge into a chorus, blend into *Black Self*. And now I can tell you, knowing that you will listen beyond these words and hear my gratitude and my love.

The Pulitzer Prize! What numerous concentric circles of meaning whirled in that triumph. A Black woman, winning the most prized Prized! And for a loving portrait of Black womanhood, thus a revelation of the essence of our People. You showed the world you/our genius. You bent to your will the poetic forms of the oppressor and on his own battlefield, you won. More important, we began to know you, and in time we claimed you as our voice.

Yet that was not the end but only the beginning. Part of a growing and a becoming. You listened to us speak and transformed our language into art. You filtered our struggles through your genius and showed us truth. You took our Selves into gentle hands and gave us back our Selves, gave us clairvoyance through which we could know our value. You gave us perfect works, like "Kitchenette Building" and "Riot," which in their perfection showed us ourselves. You gave us characters who have enriched our world— Annie Allen, Chocolate Mabbie, the eldery Bean-eaters (our grandparents, our parents, ourselves), Satin-Legs Smith, the seven cool (doomed) pool-players, Rudolph Reed, the not-lost youth of big cities—a world, our world.

And you yourself. You are the most vital character of all—you with your warm smile and soft voice and unutterable strength. Encouraging young artists with your example and, not only that, with your time and money. Being one of the supporters of OBAC, sponsoring projects like *The Black Position*, offering prizes to new writers (of which I was a proud beneficiary), publishing with a Black press, showing us the way, giving us the image of ourselves which is nothing short of revolutionary.

How can I tell it all? I am so proud to exist in this world at the same time as you, to be able to say to those who come after, "I have met her, I know her, she is a friend."

How can I tell it all? Had I the skill, I would sing as our ancestors did, piling image upon image until the listener sensed, deep within the recesses of the self, your marvelous being.

Spirit-mother of us all,
how can I sing your praise?

Gwendolyn Brooks and the Principle of Generosity: A Night in North Philly
James G. Spady

Brooks. Rivers of destiny. Streams. *Conscience*. Consciounsess. Honor. Coded persona. Mississippi. Emmett Till. Little Lincoln. Brownstone Kids. River Children. High Climbers. Blues motifed. Principles. Is it the end of the dawn or the beginning of daylight? Sixties fixed. Places. Seas of yesterfutures.

Night. It was a special night on Columbia Avenue. A snowy cold night. Library officials of the Columbia Avenue branch of the Free Library of Philadelphia advised a cancellation. Miss Brooks at the North Philly Matrix.

It was February, 1972. The shiny white snow glistened in the deeply dark night of the city. We had invited Gwendolyn Brooks out to be a part of the "Black Mu" poetry forum organized by our UMUM collective—Black History Museum Committee. Capitalized by the UMUM aggregation and the mass-based black community, there was no attractive honorarium, no coveted award, no special ceremony. There *were* time honored principles for which we stood. We were offering one of the very few public forums for black poetry in Philadelphia and we had published an anthology of Black Philadelphia Poets, *Black Poets Write On*. We were young bloods situated and saturated in this sprawling urban metropolis called Phillytown.

Gwendolyn Brooks, the Pulitzer Prize winning poet and Bronzeville lady, generously accepted our invitation, fully knowledgeable that we were not able to provide the honorarium her booking agent so vigorously suggested.

This night, Gwen entered a packed public library auditorium confounding the downtown library authorities who assured us and apprised some of their staff members that she would not be there.

Among the many poets who read that night was Rikki Lights (at the time Co-Editor of *Ra Magazine* along with Juan Williams, Washington Post columnist and author of the book, *Eyes on the Prize*). Currently a practicing physician and author of the excellent Afro-Gullah collection of poems, *Dogmoon*, Rikki was at that time a student at Bryn Mawr College. So anxious was she to read her poetry on the Black Mu Poetry Forum that a construction truck delivered her safely to this sacred spot. Aside from the poets scheduled to read, there were many who came in from the street, alert and alive with the Black Muse intact.

Gwen was moved that night. She spoke extemporaneously and joined the symphony of poets who read that evening. Some came from as far as Boston, New York City, Washington, D.C. and Lincoln University, Pa. They, too, shared generously.

Upon her return to Chicago, Gwendolyn Brooks mailed three checks ($100 per person). Two of the three recipients started publishing ventures. All of there were inspired to continue to move in a self-reliant manner. Sterling X later wrote the novel, *The Black Angels*, and assisted in editing a volume of speeches and interviews by Minister Louis Farrakhan. Jymi Jones carried the Philly spirit to Mexico, all the while writing in that "guerilla" genre so common to a sector of Philly black poetry. Eugene Howard has published widely and marvelously since that time. Beth Jackson and Patricia Ford continue to combine poetry and music.

It was Gwendolyn Brooks' operative philosophical principle of generosity (we use this term as both magnanimously and in the

Edelian scientifically philosophic sense) that led her to Columbia Avenue—site of the 1964 urban rebellion. As we write this Quadida piece for Gwendolyn Brooks, we are mindful that Columbia Avenue has been renamed for Cecil B. Moore, Esq., the baddest mass-based black leader in Philly during the 1950s and 60s. Who knows but that Miss Brooks' presence may have spawned countless persons to become poets, writers—more importantly, her principle of generosity remains an ever present memory in North Philly.

A Celebration of Life
Gwendolyn Brooks at Threescore + 10
Andrea Taylor

Few among us are able to make a work of art of life. Fewer still do so triumphantly. The radiance of such a spirit generates its own life force; a force that is self-sustaining and empowers others.

Gwendolyn Brooks believes that art should be used for liberation, not decoration. She prevails. Her work celebrates life, exposes spiritual death and offers hope for spiritual rebirth. The poet's commitment to her craft reveals truth extracted from memory, being and possibility. It is her release, but she seeks to understand, rather than to be understood.

The quality of this life transcends image. Yet it penetrates reality in sharp focus. The imagination of such a spirit is visionary. It concedes no boundaries in the universe. Ancestors are the source of strength and wisdom. History is the palette for sketches of her people. America is the canvas. These portraits offer the chance to recapture our humanity. This is the gift. The mentors dwell in the Mecca and Bronzeville, as well as in Chicago and Johannesburg.

Freedom is paramount; but must not be pursued alone. A people must go with her. In unison and with love, the prophetess knows that the quality of all life can be enriched. At the intersection of her voice and the predicament of her people, the tone is clear, the time is now.

A disciplined spirit has roots. The parents, Keziah and David, nurtured her daydreams from an early age. The long-lost memory of their love was the vessel for this work of art; the life. The creation belongs to the people now. And we rejoice in the celebration of her presence and beauty among us.

Gwendolyn Brooks Anew!
Woodie King, Jr.

As this issue celebrates your 70th birthday I look anew, with increasing admiration, upon your distinguished body of work and how that body of work defined our generation. *We Real Cool* as a theatre piece led the way into the formation of The Negro Ensemble Company; *The Sundays of Satin Legs Smith* defined for me forever what has taken sociologists hundreds of pages to describe. Few artists in this generation have been privileged to receive so many important awards as you have, and certainly few have done so with such devotion to the Black Arts. We witness again such works as *The Chicago Defender Sends a Man to Little Rock Fall, 1957*, *Annie Allen*, and *A Street in Bronzeville* — a love for Black people so strong, stereotypes would not dare intrude. Black artists are proud of you; we know you have used your great talents in the interest of all people. May you have many years of happiness and health and may we continue to have the benefit of your poetic contributions.

Some Thoughts on "Sadie and Maud"
Louis D. Mitchell

Emily Dickenson once said, "If I read a book and it makes my whole body so cold no fire can ever warm me, I know that it is poetry. If I feel physically as if the top of my head were taken off, I know that is poetry." Gwendolyn Brooks' poetry — which says that which cannot be said, to echo Edwin Arlington Robinson — is full of extraordinary chiselings with words which disclose their own essential traits, not simply that they might exist through the vicarage of words themselves. What results is a sensitive retreat to the elementary, the simply, and the very shivering life of particulars.

They might, and do, reveal their properties as workmanship—she is truly a wordsmith of extraordinary variety—for that very workmanship is a trait in which the ethical and the aesthetic are one.

For example, what is a comb in the poem, "Sadie and Maud"? The subtle technique is one of Miss Brooks' poetic ingenuities. If one were to assemble a thesaurus of all the important qualifications and meanings of the term "comb" as Miss Brooks uses them in this poem, what would the qualifications and meanings be? "Sadie scraped life/ with a fine-tooth comb," expresses one of those delicately honed observations involving a way of living, a deliberate choice of lifestyle, to be deep, glad, and complete in the process of living every moment. The comb at the same time portrays steps from something to something. It indicates a curve of development or change of lifestyle from Ma's, Maud's, and Papa's expectations or dictates.

Then Miss Brooks goes on to associate further with a comprehensive glimpse of how Sadie uses that comb. "She didn't leave a tangle in./ Her comb found every strand." Thus one pervasive quality of motivation is modified and ramified. She left no aspect of life unlived and in doing so Sadie found every crack and crevice, strain and pull of life, feeling its every impulse, its steady undercurrents. There are tenuous materials here to indicate how the avowed relation between the visible and the invisible finds variants or sophistication in the artist's, reader's and poet's appreciation. How this appreciation in an age of such intense querulousness serves rather to transcend the querulous is poignantly resolved in that Sadie had left as her heritage her fine-tooth comb. The final ironic twist to Sadie's use of that comb is that she went on away to her life, whatever it would bring, but Maud, who had gone to college, lives all alone in the old house—Ma and Papa had gone on to that world beyond the grave. The balance between Sadie and Maud, what happens to each is all spelled out in words of different weight, sizes, shapes, and orders.

Thus one sympathizes with the intention of the poet for her vision of life and its variable ingredients (a fine-tooth comb being one of them) arises out of a total view of society—a view which does not blink at the ugliness that is ever present. Thus we get an anomalous patch—the morality that Sadie protests against and subsequently violates—in this, a prevailingly blunt, animated and finely-chiseled modern examination of four lives at once which mirror the world that humanity uses and abuses. This is a world sculpted for us out of hard reality—"speech framed," as Gerard Manley Hopkins says, "to be heard for its own sake and interest even over and above its interest or meaning"—powerfully imposed on the conscious and subconscious mind. This is poetry in the truest sense of the word.

To Gwendolyn Brooks Our Sage
Warren C. Swindell

In his autobiography, Olaudah Equiano, an Eighteenth-Century victim of European greed, attests to the importance of music, dance and poetry in African culture. Throughout the continent of Africa, almost every village had musicians, dancers, and griots who created and extended powerful art forms. New-Africans in the United States continued this tradition of synthesizing experience and expressing it symbolically through their use of music, poetry and dance. The music and lyrics of the New-Africans, too, was distinctive for its vivid imagery. The calls, cries, hollers, shouts, wails, and moans, the moans, the moans, the moans of the new-Africans have travelled around the universe and back, over and over again, each time in new and richer forms.

Of our living new-African griots, we salute Gwendolyn Brooks our sage. She is our inspiration, our living link with the beautiful sisters of yesteryear...Queen Hatshepsut...Queen Tity...Nefertiti...Cleopatra...Hypatia...The Queen of Sheba...Queen Kahina...Queen Nzingha...Yaa Asantewa...the Herero Women...Harriet...Sojourner...Gwendolyn Brooks has been to the mountaintop but she remembers those of us still in the valley. She has not sold out, $$$ *Ask your Mama* $$$.

Our house pet writers and poets express one dimension of the new-African experience, but the true essence is not to be found in the experience of the house pets. Gwendolyn tells us of our experience in the baptist, methodist, holiness, santified, and pentecostal black churches, the blues, jazz, soul, and rap houses, the streets, the foundaries, the packing houses, the auto assembly plants, the penitentiaries, and the housing projects. Gwen is our consciousness, our contact with reality. We at Indiana State University love you Gwen.

For Gwendolyn Brooks
Delores Lipscomb

You write about everyday occurrences and ordinary people. Some of your subjects: the poor, the carefree, the unborn, the holy and the hustler. Not much of the urban ghetto has escaped your acute vision.

Simplicity, normality and naturalness characterize your verse and yield its power. Hidden beneath the seemingly normal speech patterns lie formal rhythmic structures creating emphasis and hammering the message to the reader. This forward motion captures the reader's mental ear as the meaning and the music become one.

And what of the musical sounds? The sounds of "We Real Cool, Lurk late, Strike straight, Sing sin, Think gin, Jazz June, Die soon. The blending of the consonants and vowels with the rhythm and the variations of grammatical structure create verbal echoes of events leading to these youngsters' early deaths. But the right combination of words and phrases, rhythms and sounds, produce the mental music that empowers the reader to store the dancing images forever.

You are the master writer, the crafter of words and language. You are the poet, the maker of meaning and music.

For all aspiring writers searching to produce the perfect blend of form and idea, the quest ends here.

On Gwendolyn's Poem, "The Mother"
Toks Pearse

At the core of this poem is the notion of the responsibility of womanhood. It is a monologue and a lament of one woman which ultimately transcends the worries of one person and becomes the agony of a community, even of humanity.

A murder has been committed, a child is killed, human blood has been spilled and leaves a trail of guilt "abortions will not let you forget." Human life has been deprived of life, deprived of a future, even of a real presence.

Murder is bad enough, but what manner of woman would poison the umbilical cord of her own children? This woman's lament is heart-rending. Her admission of guilt is evidence of her extreme pain. "I have heard in the voices of the wind the voices of my dim killed children" — "If I poisoned the beginnings of your breaths, Believe that even in my deliberateness I was not deliberate." Now she has no children to play with, no one with whom to reciprocate love, care, tears of joy and tears of sorrow—all the experience of wanting and being wanted—an enriched experience of being.

Gwendolyn Brooks is a poet of the people hence explication of her poems must be sought from race-communal perspectives. "The Mother" is about individual pain, but the poem also strikes a chord on the matriarchy of African antiquity. As the Sotho of South Africa say, "touch the women and you strike the rock of the land." In the same spirit of maternal potency, the Yoruba people of Nigeria assert, "Iyani wura, omo lowo" — "Mother is gold, and children, the currency wrought from its ore." African societies view maternity as a blessing from the gods. In support of that belief, African literature is replete with the notion that barrenness is a woman's payback for evil sorcery.

African-American history and culture have kept this traditional belief alive. The female is central to society. She is not as in the Greco-Roman tradition some helpless victim of a male dominated world; a child who must be protected from the real world. The African woman is viewed by her society as a provider, a leader, responsible for herself, often responsible also for her men-folk. When she is presented as a victim, we know that her helplessness is not intrinsic to her nature, rather one that is imposed by a temporarily victorious assailant.

For a people plagued by the fear of communal disintegration, and for a people who live in a communal environment where manual family labor is key to economic survival, children are precious and motherhood revered. This is the cultural backcloth from which Gwendolyn Brooks fashions her poem. So in reading this poem, we are compelled to ask ourselves: What manner of woman would destroy her own life-line, stop the flow of life in its tracks and commit such a dastardly crime against nature? What type of woman is "The Mother" who will not mother her children, but would rather murder them. The genius of Gwendolyn Brooks is her ability to let the reader see that "The Mother," a self-confessed fetus killer is not a common criminal, but a sensitive woman overwhelmed by the politics of experience.

Miz Brooks, Thank You
Collette Armstead

The first time I met Ms. Brooks was in 1980. I had read an article in the *Chicago Sun-Times* about how the "Black Bard" was encouraging young writers to write. Thinking that I was young (I was twenty-one) and I wanted to be a writer I assumed she would help me. She was speaking at Roosevelt University. I gathered up my poems, pen, paper and courage and went to see her.

I was so excited about the event that I arrived 2 hours early. I sat in the Roosevelt lounge. I paced. Around a half-hour before the reading was to begin, I walked towards the hall where it was being held. The lecture room was beginning to fill. The surrounding corridors were crowded with students and visitors. I loitered through the halls. As I walked I noticed a dark-skinned older woman sitting serenely in a chair. "That's Gwendolyn Brooks," I thought as I walked past her. I turned around and walked past her again peering into her face trying not to be too obvious. The hall was filled and there were people of all ages and colors milling around. No one recognized her. After I had walked past her three or four times I put my heart in my mouth and approached. "Uh, maam, are you...Gwendolyn Brooks?" "Yes," she replied. "Uh, Miz Brooks, my name is Collette Armstead. I-I write. I mean, I think I'm a writer. I've been writing..." My brief speech was taking forever to say. Ms. Brooks handed me a sheet of paper with her address written on it. "Here's my address," she said, "write me a letter." "Thank you, Miz Brooks. I will."

Soon after our exchange a University official escorted Ms. Brooks into the lecture hall. I followed and found what had to be the last seat in the auditorium. I can't recall all she read that night, but I do remember "To My Sisters Who Kept Their Naturals." I was very proud of my natural hair and very proud to have been in her presence.

The next day I sat down and composed a very embarrassing, confusing, ten-page letter. I put aside how foolish I felt and mailed it.

One month later I had a response and an autographed copy of *Primer for Young Poets*. The note gave me the address of OBAC Writers Workshop. I promised myself to be at the Worshop's next meeting.

Three years later, when I was accepted as a member of the workshop, I sent a very concise and syrupy note of thanks to Ms. Brooks.

In 1987, as part of an internship award given to me by the University I attend, I worked out of the South Side Community Art Center for OBAC under apprenticeship as a cultural manager. The receptionist, Kim, a fellow student at Northeastern Illinois University asked me for a copy of a poem I had written about a "shapphire blue peacock who could fly, while lifting the load of riches while mute skies watched." Kim loved the poem and her grandmother lived down the block from Ms. Brooks-Blakely. Kim showed the poem to her grandmother's neighbor and Ms. Brooks sent back words of encouragement and a message to keep writing. I thought another letter might be appropriate, but got swet up in the whirlwind of school, work and family.

At the end of 1986 I was an arts management trainee at Business Volunteers for the Arts (BVA). BVA is a not-for-profit arts service organization that provides a skills bank for arts organizations. BVA was in the midst of an earned income project with Marshall Field's and Divine Cookie Company. Divines was creating a Chicago Edition of their product; a hand-made fortune cookie with literary fortunes inside. The Executive Director asked if I could arrange for Gwendolyn Brooks to lend her name and excerpts of her poetry to the campaign. I would try.

Ms. Brooks was reading at Columbia College the next night. I arranged to meet Angela Jackson (OBAC's Chairperson) and have her reintroduce me to Ms. Brooks. (A word about the reading that night. Ms. Brooks took the audience of poets and students, plucked the feathers from our wings, laid them gently in the palm of her hand and blew ever so gently. In other words, she blew us away with power and majesty.)

After the reading, I waited until most everyone who was going to talk with her had left. I placed the brightly colored folder that held the presentation in my hand and made my pitch. She listened and turned to Angela. "Is she a good poet?" she asked. Angela nodded. "Anything you'd like to use is fine," she said. I was stunned. She had given me Carte Blanche. I had thought of all the things to say if she turned me down but nothing if she had accepted. Another poet came and Ms. Brooks talked to the artist as she walked towards the door.

While walking in the warm December air with Angela down Wabash, I turned to her and said, "Angela, I am so rude and ungrateful. I forgot to tell Mizz Brooks thank you."

This is my opportunity.

Miz Brooks,

Thank you.

Gwendolyn Brooks:
Jean Toomer's November Cotton Flower
Joyce Ann Joyce

As epigraph to Part I of her very important book *When and Where I Enter: The Impact of Black Women on Race and Sex in America*, Paula Giddings cites Toni Morrison's evaluation of her character Sula. Morrison says, "...she |Sula| had nothing to fall back on; not maleness, not whiteness, not ladyhood, not anything. And out of the profound desolation of her reality she may well have invented herself." Despite the nurturing and encouragement Gwendolyn Brooks received from her mother who was responsible for the young Gwen's meeting and receiving the help of James Weldon Johnson and Langston Hughes, despite the fact that her work appeared in two anthologies by the time she was twenty, despite the fact that Langston Hughes dedicated several newspaper columns and a book of short stories to her, despite the fact that Gwendolyn Brooks has received at least nine literary awards including a Pulitzer and two Guggenheims, despite the fact that she has served as poetry consultant for the Library of Congress, Gwendolyn Brooks, a Black American woman poet, had no choice but to invent herself. She has emerged as one of America's most distinguished poetic voices in spite of the history of racism and sexism that characterizes all levels of American society. Whereas it was little short of a miracle that Phillis Wheatley could read at all, perhaps it is equally miraculous that Black women pioneers like Sojourner Truth, Harriet Tubman, Ida B. Wells, Frances Harper, Mary Church Terrell, Charlotte Hawkins Brown, and Eva Bowles were successful at inventing themselves. For in their struggles to combat the impact of racism and sexism on the lives of Black women, they had no history of Black women predecessors to serve as role models to guide them. Analogously, Gwendolyn Brooks's eleven books of poetry, her novel, her autobiography, and the critical acclaim that now enthusiastically affirms her work rose out of the dearth of an American landscape hostile to the social, economic, and emotional well-being as well as the creative productivity of the Black American woman.

Against America's historical background which attempts to stiffle the spirit and creativity of the Black woman, Gwendolyn Brooks has evolved with the same beauty and impact as the flower in Jean Toomer's "November Cotton Flower":

> Boll-weevil's coming, and the winter's cold,
> Made cotton stalks look rusty, seasons old,
> And cotton, scarce as any southern snow,
> Was vanishing; the branch, so pinched and slow,
> Failed in its function as the autumn rake;
> Drouth fighting soil had caused the soil to take
> All water from the streams; dead birds were found
> In wells a hundred feet below the ground—
> Such was the season when the flower bloomed.
> Old folks were startled, and it soon assumed
> Significance. Superstition saw
> Something it had never seen before:
> Brown eyes that loved without a trace of fear,
> Beauty so sudden for that time of year.

Gwendolyn Brooks began to bloom in a season when the literary scene was even more dominated by white males than it is today. Like the cotton flower, she struggle against the drought of male censorship from one of her own kind. When Richard Wright, serving as reviewer for Harper and Brothers, negatively critiqued the poem "the mother" from *A Street in Bronzeville* because of its emphasis on abortion, he evidenced the kind of male misunderstanding of issues that effect the lives of women. Yet rather than yield to the aridity of Wright's limitations, Gwendolyn Brooks, like the strong flower which fights the deadening effects of the cold natural world, explained to editor Edward Aswell that the emphasis in her poem is not so much abortion as it is the poverty and environmental conditions that produced ambivalence in the mother's attitude toward being a parent. Interestingly enough, Wright, who moved to Paris so that his daughters could escape the stifling effects of racism in American society, failed to grasp the essence of "the mother."

Wife, mother, nurturer of her parents, poet, leader of poetry workshops, and bearer of monetary gifts to young poets, Gwendolyn Brooks assumed her own significance. Her brown/black eyes captured "without a trace of fear" the complexity of being a Black woman in America when the mainstream American poetry arena was dominated by demigods like T.S. Eliot, John Crowe Ransom, Robert Penn Warren, Allen Tate, Randall Jarrell, e.e. cummings, Karl Shapiro, and Stanley Kunitz. Having bloomed under the light of Robert Hillyer's *First Principles of Verse*, Brooks brought to modern American poetry her own peculiar sensibility which manifests at once the embodiments of both Wallace Steven's blue guitar and the African griot's drum. Even though they have the visual and stylistic attributes of a Euro-American poetic tradition, her earlier ballads, free verse poems, and the sonnets reveal the same feelings of racial integrity and record the same malaises of racism as those poems published after 1967 when Brooks's blackness confronted her "with a shrill spelling of itself." Yet this blackness, Brooks's absorption of the psychic patterns of her ancestral heritage, has made its identifiable mark on all her poetry.

Despite its use of medieval and Renaissance language to evoke the chivalric mood, "The Anniad," found in Brooks's second volume *Annie Allen*, shares with the poem "To Black Women" from *To the Diaspora*, Brooks's tenth volume, a strong ending which suggests the Black woman's resolute will to survive. One strongly, stylistically Euro-American and the other distinctly Afro-American, both poems channel the experiences of the poet's cultural heritage through the blue guitar of her creative imagination, producing complementary visions of Black women in American society. These poems looked at together serve as a single example of how Gwendolyn Brooks's poetry provide rich insights into the diversity and fluidity of the Black experience. Even though her works reveal a sharpened consciousness in the late 1960s, Gwendolyn Brooks has always been a Black priestess of words who conjured up herself by absorbing the best of the Euro-American poetic tradition and assimilating this tradition into her indigenous Black cultural experience.

She began this formidable task at a time when it was not only far from fashionable, but also iconoclastic for a Black woman to dare to infiltrate the modern American poetry arena. Thus "folks were startled." Nonetheless, the November Cotton Flower, like Jean Toomer before her, demonstrated majestically how racial themes become an element of the Black writer's craft. The end result of the merger of imitative techniques characteristic of a Euro-American tradition with the Black priestess's peculiarly Afro-American stylistic innovations thrusts Gwendolyn Brooks, a Black American woman poet, to the forefront of the American literary scene. Put simply, this Black woman writer, who had no role models to follow and who began writing at a time when it was customary for the Black writer to borrow the master's tools, reshaped those tools and made them yield to the magic of her ancestral heritage. Even though thirty-seven years have passed since Brooks received the Pulitzer Prize and even though she has served as an inspiration and teacher to many Black women poets who follow her, the historical significance of her contribution and what she symbolizes remain "Beauty so sudden for |this| time of year."

Afterward
Mari Evans

We walk, it seems, with too little wonder in the company of those of magnitude and bond, familiar sensibilities without the splash and splatter, the facile rodomontade. Full of ourselves we sometimes forget that modesty can afford a quiet generosity. An unassuming woman, this Gwendolyn Brooks to whom so much is due, from whom so much has been realized. Neighborwoman in the world; her simple offering—a lifetime's harvest.

Another poet once said of this gentlebrown woman whose insistent eyes challenge one's every move, that she would never need to look for a theme; Brooks remarked of herself that the work she is doing "requires" a big city as background. Somewhere within that meld is the distillate that nourishes Gwendolyn Brooks the Black creative artist, the wife/mother who in 1950 accepted with certain grace and composure the first Pulitzer awarded a Black artist for poetry, the sage who during the tumultuous times in the Sixties, sat attentively and unassumingly in the midst of Chicago's Blackstone Rangers offering poetry, and receiving a Ph.D. in street.

Serious appraisal and recognition of the work of African American women writers has been a long time coming. Brooks, whose career owes its longevity to the undeniable preeminence of her craftswomanship, has been an almost singular, notable exception. Staying power bought with expertise and versatility. She is at once sum and segment, tender, tenacious, terrible—to which this volume is appropriate testament.

For us this is merely seized opportunity; it is she who does us honor.

Acknowledgments and Biographical Notes

Grateful acknowledgment is made to the contributors in this volume. This book was published as a seventieth birthday surprise for Gwendolyn Brooks. A general "call" letter for submissions went out in February of 1987. We received over 300 selections from poets, writers, and artists representing many cultures. Our selections were based upon the guidelines set forth in that "call" letter and the literary quality of the work. We could not publish all of the submissions and we would like to thank all of those people who took the time to send us their work. Due to a time factor, we were unable to get back to contributors to obtain full biographies. A special thanks to Larry Dunn for his unselfish attention.

HRM

Jeanette Adams is a former student of Ms. Brooks and author of *Sukari, Love Lyrics* and *Picture Me a Poem.*

Fatimah Afif lives in Philadelphia and has studied poetry with Sonia Sanchez.

Fareedah Allah is a Washington, D.C.-based poet and activist.

Estella Conwill Alexander, Ph.D., is assistant professor of English at Kentucky State University and author of several books of poetry.

Jahari Amini is author of *Images In Black, Black Essence, Let's Go Somewhere* and *Common Sense Approach to Eating.*

Collette Armstead is program director of the Organization of Black American Cutlure Writer's Workshop.

Molefi Asante, Ph.D., is chairman of African-American Studies at Temple University. He is the author of twenty-three books, including *Afrocentricity, Rhetoric of Black Revolution* and *Transracial Communication.*

Lerone Bennett, Jr., is an internationally respected historican and author of *Before the Mayflower, The Challenge of Blackness, Confrontation: Black and White, The Negro Mood, Pioneers in Protest* and other works. He is a senior editor at *Ebony.*

William Beyer works out of Belvidere, Il.

Henry Blakely, poet, is author of *Windy Place, SectorPlan* and husband of Ms. Brooks.

Nora Brooks Blakely is a writing consultant, director of Chocolate Chips Theatre Co., and daughter of Ms. Brooks.

Randson C. Boykin is a former intern with the National Endownment for the Arts and a former member of Gwendolyn Brooks' workshop.

Walter Bradford, poet and director of St. Lenord's House in Chicago, is a former member of the Gwendolyn Brooks's workshop.

Abena Joan Brown is the co-founder and president of ETA Creative Arts Foundation in Chicago, IL. In the 1984-85 season, ETA produced a critically acclaimed original musical-drama—"A Cosmic Night" by Ernest McCarty—based on the work of Gwendolyn Brooks.

Dennis Brutus is a well known poet form South Africa. He is director of the African Studies Department at the University of Pittsburg and author of several books.

Margaret Burroughs is a visual artist, writer, and founder and director emeritus of the DuSable Museum in Chicago. She is currently a commissioner of parks for the Chicago Park District. Dr. Burroughs is a long-time friend of Gwendolyn Brooks.

Addo Carpenter is a Chicago photographer.

Barbara Cochran is a poet and a member of the Organization of Black American Culture Writer's workshop in Chicago.

Eugenia Collier, Ph.D., is professor of literature at Howard University. She is co-editor with Richard Long of *Afro American Writing*.

Linda Cousins is the publisher/editor of *The Universal Black Writer Press* of New York.

Dawn R. Crump is a Philadelphia poet.

Mari Evans is an internationally respected poet, writer and editor. Her many works include *I Am a Black Woman, Nightstar, Where Is All the Music?, Black Women Writers (1950-1980): A Critical Evaluation* and *Jim Flying High.*

Bibhas R. De writes out of La Habra, California.

Rutt Dennis writes from Virginia Commonwealth University, Richmond, Va.

Sherman L. Fowler works with the Eugene B. Redmond Writer's Workshop in East St. Louis, Mo.

Zack Gilbert, poet, is author of *My Own Hallelujahs.*

R. Nyatau Glasco is a poet writing from Camden, New Jersey.

Vivian V. Gordon, Ph.D., poet and author of *Black Women.*

Sharon Leonard Goodman is a poet working with Sonia Sanchez's Larry Neal Poetry Workshop in Philadelphia.

Stephen E. Henderson, Ph.D., is coauthor of *The Militant Black Writer*, editor of *Understanding the New Black Poetry* and professor of English at Howard University.

Fred L. Hord, poet and author of *After Hours*, teaches at Howard University.

Amelia Blossom House is a South African poet in exile in the United States.

Angela Jackson is the author of *VooDoo/Love Magic* and *Solo in the Boxcar Third Floor E, A House of Extended Families* and is the guiding spirit of Chicago's OBAC Writers' Workshop.

Sandra Jackson-Opoku, award-winning writer and member of OBAC. She is the author of *A Language of Lions*.

Joyce Ann Joyce, Ph.D., is the author of *Native Son: Richard Wright's Art of Tragedy*. She is an associate professor at the University of Maryland.

Kathleen M. Kemmerer's poetry has appeared in the *San Fernando Poetry Journal, Instress* and *Speculum.*

Woodie King Jr. is founder and producer of the New Federal Theatre at Henry Street Settlement in New York City. He is also a director, an editor, and author of *Black Theatre Present Condition.*

Shirley Bradley LeFlore is a poet and community activist from St. Louis, Mo.

Roy Lewis is a Washington, D.C., photographer who literally paints with his camera. He has capture the recent history of Black people on film.

Robert Lima, poet and translator. His versions of Hispanic poems have appeared in many journals. He is the author of *Fathoms* and *The Olde Ground.*

Delores Lipscomb, Ph.D., co-editor of *Tapping Potential.* She is professor of English at Chicago State University.

Naomi Long Madgett, publisher/editor of Lotus Press. She is author of *Pink Ladies in the Afternoon, Songs to A Phantom Nightgale, One and the Many, Star By Star* and other books.

Haki R. Madhubuti, poet, publisher, editor and educator. His is the author of fifteen books of poetry, criticism, and essays. His latest work of poetry is *Killing Memory, Seeking Ancestors*. He is an associate professor of English at Chicago State Universitiy.

Ginger Mance is a Chicago poet.

Thad Mathis is a member of Sonia Sanchez's poetry workshop in Philadelphia.

D.H. Melhem is poet and author of *Gwendolyn Brooks: The Heroic Voice.*

Gwendolyn Mitchell is a poet writing from Dallas, Texas.

Louis D. Mitchell writes from Scranton, Pennsylvania.

Dorothea M. Moore writes from Newark, New Jersey.

Lenord D. Moore writes from Raleigh, North Carolina.

Maria K. Mootry, poet and scholar, has written a critical study of Gwendolyn Brooks's poetry.

Sisi Donald Mosby is a writer, journalist and host of NPR radio program *Tales of Chicago.*

Akua Serwaa Omowale is on the faculty of California State University at Long Beach.

Raymond R. Patterson is a major poet writing from New York. He is the author of many books.

Toks Pearse, Ph.D., is a Nigerian writer who has published criticism and articles in England. He coordinates the University Without Walls Program at Chicago State University.

Useni Eugene Perkins, poet, playwright, and sociologist. Author of *Home Is A Dirty Street* and the recent *Harvesting New Generations.*

Sterling Plumpp, award-winning poet and author of *Half Black, Half Blacker, Black Rituals, Steps to Break the Circle, The Mojo Hands Call, I Must Go* and other works.

Robert Earl Price writes from Atlanta, Georgia.

Eugene B. Redmond is an award-winning poet, editor and scholar. He is the author of *Drum Voices: The Mission of Afro-American Poetry, Sentry of the Four Golden Pillars, River of Bones and Flesh and Blood* and other books.

Sonia Sanchez is an internationally respected poet and playwright. She is a professor of English at Temple University and the author of numerous books including *Homecoming, Generations, I've Been A Woman* and others.

A. Oliver Shands writes from Peekskill, New York.

Saundra Sharp is a poet and actor working out of Los Angeles. She has been in the forefront of the struggle for correct Black images in the mass media.

James G. Spady, historian, researcher and scholar, has been a major actor in the struggle for African and African-American studies in the United States.

Warren C. Swindell is Director of the Center for Afro-American Studies at Indiana State University.

Andrea Taylor is a journalist and an entrepeneur in Cleveland, Ohio.

Askia M. Touré, poet, political activist, is co-editor of a forthcoming journal, *Black Voices*.

Eleanor Traylor, Ph.D., is a professor of English at Montgomery College in Rockville, Maryland. She frequently lectures within and outside the United States on Afro-American literary traditions.

Sandra West writes from Montclair, New Jersey.

Kimmika L.H. Williams is the television editor for *Maceba Affairs* magazine.

Alfred L. Woods is the author of *Mannish*. He resides in Chicago.

Stephen Caldwell Wright is the author of *Poems In Movement* and is on the faculty of Seminole Community College.

Beryl Zitch, long-time friend and literary agent for Ms. Brooks.

Sander Zulauf writes from Succasunna, New Jersey.

ALSO AVAILABLE FROM THIRD WORLD PRESS

Nonfiction

The Destruction Of Black Civilization: Great Issues Of A Race From 4500 B.C. To 2000 A.D.
by Dr. Chancellor Williams
paper $16.95
cloth $29.95

The Cultural Unity Of Black Africa
by Cheikh Anta Diop $14.95

Confusion By Any Other Name
edited by Haki Madhubuti $3.95

Home Is A Dirty Street
by Useni Eugene Perkins $9.95

Isis Papers
by Francis Cress Welsing
paper $14.95
cloth $29.95

Reconstructing Memory
by Fred L. Hord $12.95

Black Men: Obsolete, Single, Dangerous?
by Haki R. Madhubuti
paper $14.95
cloth $29.95

From Plan To Planet Life Studies: The Need For Afrikan Minds And Institutions
by Haki R. Madhubuti $7.95

Enemies: The Clash Of Races
by Haki R. Madhubuti $12.95

Kwanzaa: A Progressive And Uplifting African-American Holiday
by Institute of Positive Education
Intro. by Haki R. Madhubuti $2.50

Harvesting New Generations: The Positive Development Of Black Youth
by Useni Eugene Perkins $12.95

Explosion Of Chicago Black Street Gangs
by Useni Eugene Perkins $6.95

The Psychopathic Racial Personality And Other Essays
by Dr. Bobby E. Wright $5.95

Black Women, Feminism And Black Liberation: Which Way?
by Vivian V. Gordon $5.95

Black Rituals
by Sterling Plumpp $8.95

The Redemption Of Africa And Black Religion
by St. Clair Drake $6.95

How I Wrote Jubilee
by Margaret Walker $1.50

A Lonely Place Against The Sky
by Dorothy Palmer Smith $7.95

Fiction

Mostly Womenfolk And A Man Or Two: A Collection
by Mignon Holland Anderson $5.95

The Brass Bed and Other Stories
Pearl Cleage $8.00

Poetry and Drama
To Disembark
by Gwendolyn Brooks $6.95

I've Been A Woman
by Sonia Sanchez $7.95

My One Good Nerve
by Ruby Dee $8.95

Geechies
by Gregory Millard $5.95

Earthquakes And Sunrise Missions
by Haki R. Madhubuti $8.95

So Far, So Good
by Gil-Scott Heron $8.00

Killing Memory: Seeking Ancestors
(Lotus Press)
by Haki R. Madhubuti $8.00

Say That The River Turns:
The Impact Of Gwendolyn Brooks
(Anthology)
Ed.by Haki R. Madhubuti $8.95

Octavia And Other Poems
by Naomi Long Madgett $8.00

A Move Further South
by Ruth Garnett $7.95

Manish
by Alfred Woods $8.00

New Plays for the Black Theatre
(Anthology)
edited by Woodie King, Jr. $14.95

Wings Will Not Be Broken
Darryl Holmes $8.00

Sortilege (Black Mystery)
by Abdias do Nascimento $2.95

Children's Books
The Day They Stole
The Letter J
by Jabari Mahiri $3.95

The Tiger Who Wore
White Gloves
by Gwendolyn Brooks $6.95

A Sound Investment
by Sonia Sanchez $2.95

Afrocentric Self Inventory and
Discovery Workbook
by Useni Perkins $5.95

I Look At Me
by Mari Evans $2.50

The Story of Kwanzaa
by Safisha Madhubuti $5.95

Black Books Bulletin
A limited number of back issues
of this unique journal are available
at $3.00 each:

Vol. 1, Fall '71	Interview with Hoyt W. Fuller
Vol. 1, No. 3	Interview with Lerone Bennett, Jr.
Vol. 5, No. 3	Science & Struggle
Vol. 5, No. 4	Blacks & Jews
Vol. 7, No. 3	The South

ALSO AVAILABLE FROM THIRD WORLD PRESS

Order from **Third World Press,** 7524 S. Cottage Grove Ave. Chicago, IL 60619. Shipping: Add $2.50 for first book and .50 for each additional book. Mastercard/Visa orders may be placed by calling 1(312) 651-0700.